Boeing Super Hornet & Growler

F/A-18E/F – EA-18G

Hugh Shrakin

Boeing Super Hornet & Growler
F/A-18E/F - EA-18G

© Hugh Shrakin 2014

Published by Centurion Publishing
United Kingdom

ISBN 10: 1-903630-36-5
ISBN 13: 978-1-903630-36-5

This volume first published in 2014

The Author is identified as the copyright holder of this work under sections 77 and 78 of the Copyright Designs and Patents Act 1988

Cover design © Centurion Publishing & Createspace

Page layout, concept and design © Centurion Publishing

The traditional start of chapter on the recto side only has been intentionally disregarded; chapters starting on either the recto or versa side as required in the interests of the environment

All rights reserved. No part of this publication may be reproduced, stored in a retrieval system, transmitted in any form, or by any means, electronic, mechanical or photocopied, recorded or otherwise, without the written permission of the Publisher

The Publisher and Author would like to thank all organisations and services for their assistance and contributions in the preparation of this volume. In particular The Boeing Company, General Electric Aircraft Engines, NASA Dryden Flight Research Centre, NASA Langley Research Centre, Northrop Grumman, Raytheon, USAF, US Department of Defence, USN, USMC, US Naval Air Warfare Centre-Weapons Division/Aircraft Division, USN F-18 Advanced Weapons Laboratory and the RAAF

CONTENTS

Introduction	4
Chapter 1: First Generation Hornet	5
Chapter 2: Super Hornet Genesis	16
Chapter 3: Super Hornet Described	28
Chapter 4: Super Hornet Engineering & Manufacturing Development Phase	69
Chapter 5: Into Production	93
Chapter 6: Super Hornet Operational Evaluation	98
Chapter 7: Super Hornet in Service	102
Chapter 8: EA-18G Growler and Advanced Super Hornet	124
Chronology	137
Appendices	141
Glossary	142

F/A-18F1 lands on-board during carrier qualifications. Boeing

INTRODUCTION

The Boeing F/A-18E/F Super Hornet program was born out of a requirement to find a replacement for the cancelled A-12 Avenger II strike aircraft and, through various twists and turns, it became an Grumman F-14 Tomcat replacement and would supplement the smaller, less capable, F/A-18C/D in USN service. Conducting its first flight in prototype form in 1995, Production deliveries commenced in 1998 and the aircraft entered full operational service in the first years of the 21st Century. As well as being the USN's premier strike fighter, the F/A-18F is also operated the Royal Australian Air Force, deliveries commencing in 2010.

The EA-18G Growler was developed as a replacement for the EA-6B Prowler in the electronic warfare role. The prototype was flown in 2006 and the Growler achieved initial operational capability in 2009.

The Super Hornet has a number of pluses and minuses, but the bottom line is that the aircraft can do the job it was designed for and has potential for future growth as evidenced by the emergence of the Advanced Super Hornet, a growth development of the Block II Super Hornet, primarily aimed at increasing range and reducing the aircraft's radar signature. In the Boeing F/A-18E/F Super Hornet the USN got the aircraft that they asked for; no 'silver bullet', but an affordable evolution from the F/A-18C/D Hornet.

This volume recounts the Super Hornet and Growler programs genesis and development and describes the aircraft and systems along with entry into service details, with an overview of customer usage and potential future growth in the shape of the Advanced Super Hornet which emerged in 2013. All facts and figures used in the preparation of this volume come from official sources such as manufacturers, operators, government agencies and test organisations.

Chapter 1

FIRST GENERATION HORNET

An F/A-18C, armed with Sidewinder and AMRAAM air to air missiles as well as a cluster bomb and an AGM-88 HARM, catapults from the deck of a carrier. DoD

Before any study of the Boeing F/A-18E/F Super Hornet and EA-18G Growler is looked at in any detail it would first of all be pertinent to take a brief look at the first generation Hornet which led to the larger Super Hornet. Arguably the most versatile multi-role warplane of its era, the Boeing (formerly McDonnell Douglas) F/A-18 Hornet was developed from the Northrop YF-17 Cobra, which made its first flight 9 June 1974. Following its defeat in the USAF LWF (Lightweight Fighter), later ACF (Air Combat Fighter), competition to the General Dynamics YF-16 in January 1975, a developed Cobra emerged victorious against the YF-16 in the USN/USMC (United States Navy/United States Marine Corp) Naval ACF program four months later. The developed Cobra variant was developed by McDonnell Douglas as the F/A-18 and selected by the USN as its future NACF originally known as the VFAX.

While the USN Navy was pressured to select the winner of the USAF ACF competition, it favoured the developed variant of the YF-17 for its twin-engine safety. The F/A-18, named Hornet, was designed as a more sophisticated derivative of the land based YF-17, optimised for the carrier landing environment. The Hornet was originally to be built in two versions: F-18 for fighter/interception and A-18 for the strike/attack role. Eventually a common airframe was designed to undertake all roles, thus the multi-role F/A-18 was born.

The Hornet, like the Cobra before it, was a twin-engine, twin fin aircraft with a modestly swept wing with leading-edge manoeuvre flaps, trailing edge-flaps inboard and ailerons outboard, together with all moving tailplanes, all controlled by a digital FBW (Fly-By-Wire) flight control system. Symmetrical tailplane movement provides pitch control while differential movement is used for roll control. The inboard flaps function as flaperons during low speed flight. A single large door type airbrake is situated between the two vertical tail fins.

The first generation Hornet was directly derived from the Northrop YF-17, the losing contender in the USAF Lightweight Fighter competition. The second of the YF-17's was later transferred to the NASA Dryden Flight Research Centre and is seen here during a flight from Dryden in 1976. NASA DFRC

The single-main wheel undercarriage units retract to lie in the fuselage and the twin nose wheel unit retracts forward to lie in the forward fuselage below the cockpit. To facilitate stowage in the confined space of the carriers hanger deck the Hornets outer wing panel can be folded upwards through 100 degrees at the inboard edge of each aileron. The wing folding is powered by an AiResearch mechanical drive. In order to ease maintenance the Hornet has 268 access panels, 238 of which can be reached from ground level.

A land based version of the aircraft with the designation F-18L was to have been built for export customers. Under an agreement between McDonnell Douglas Corporation (MDC) and Northrop, MDC received design leadership and the larger work-share of the navalised F/A-18, while Northrop had design leadership and the larger work-share of the land based F-18L. However, the land based F-18L was never built, export customers instead opting for the navalised F/A-18, ensuring a degree of commonality with the USN. Another factor in the selection of the F/A-18 over the F-18L by export customers was the unwillingness of many nations to become launch customer for the F-18L. This caused disagreement between the two partners resulting in Northrop filing a lawsuit against MDC, the disagreements, which were resolved, did not seriously effect development of the aircraft.

The F/A18A/B Hornet was powered by a pair of General Electric F404-GE-400 low by-pass turbofan engines each rated at 71.2-kN (16,000-lb) with afterburner. This powerplant was developed from the YJ101 turbofan which powered the YF-17 Cobra. The -400 powerplant was continued as standard when production of the F/A-18C/D began. In January 1992, production switched to Block 36 with the F404-GE-402 EPE (Enhanced Performance Engine) rated at 78.3-kN (17,600-lb)

Australia was the first export customer for the F/A-18, the Royal Australian Air Force receiving 57 F/A-18A's and 18 F/A-18B's, the first aircraft being delivered in October 1984. This mid-life upgraded F/A-18B is armed with ASRAAM air to air missiles. MBDA

with afterburner. Some earlier productions F/A-18C/D's received the new powerplant as a retrofit. Air is fed to the engines by simple 'D' shaped fixed-geometry intakes.

Three multi-functions display screens dominated the F/A-18's cockpit and HOTAS (Hands on Throttle and Stick) controls operate all vital combat functions. The Hughes (now Raytheon) AN/APG-65 radar was at the heart of the Hornet's capability, enabling it to undertake interception, strike/attack or defence suppression missions on a single sortie at the flick of a switch; a capability often termed 'swing role'. The other dominant feature in the cockpit is the Kaiser AN/AVQ-28 HUD (Head-Up Display) which displays all the relevant weapon aiming and flight information at eye level.

The most important sensor is the AN/APG-65 multi-mode radar, which is equally effective in the air to air and air to surface role, and for a generation was the standard that other radar designers had to beat. From June 1994, new build FA-18C/D's were delivered with the APG-73 radar, which is based on the APG-65. The new radar has an increased performance processor and wider bandwidth receiver exciter in order to support future growth.

The standard F/A-18 EW (Electronic Warfare) suite consists of a Litton ALR-67(V)2 RWR (Radar Warning Receiver) and the Sanders ALQ-126B internal jammer. USN plans were for the installation of an improved RWR, the ALR-67(V)3 Advanced Special Receiver in its F/A-18C/D's. Canadian and Spanish aircraft additionally have the ALQ-162 continuous wave radar jammer

Canada was the second Hornet export customer. This CF-18A is over Macedonian during Operation Allied Force in 1999. USAF

F-18A NASA tail number 840 served as the F-18 HARV (High Alpha Research Vehicle) from 1987 until 1996, during which it received a thrust-vectoring system. The aircraft is over the mountains of southern California during a 1994 flight. NASA DFRC

As part of the development contract a batch of 11 pre-production aircraft consisting of 9 single-seat F-18A's and two twin-seat F-18B's (the YF-18 designations often referred to were unofficial designations as the aircraft were not prototypes but pre-production aircraft) were ordered for trials, the first of which flew on 18 November 1978, with all eleven aircraft flying by March 1980.

At the time of its arrival the F/A-18 was equipped with the most advanced fighter cockpit in the world. Its Hughes AN/APG-65 radar and AIM-7 Sparrow Medium range semi-active radar guided air to air missile capability put it way ahead of the rival F-16, which in its initial versions, had no beyond visual range air to air capability. On the down side the Hornet was 'short legged', a problem that arose all too often during its development.

The USN was overtly enthusiastic about the Hornet and was anxious to get its new fighter into service to replace the remaining MDC F-4 Phantom II and LTV (Vought) A-7 Corsairs II's. However, there was concern that the Hornet could not carry as heavy a load or fly as far as any of the two aircraft it was replacing, and was also limited in its 'bring back' capability when landing on the carrier deck with normal fuel reserve.

Before entering full-scale service the Hornet was evaluated by the USN Test Squadron VX-5, which recommended that the Hornet program be suspended until a solution to the range and 'bring back' problems could be found. VX-5's recommendations fell on deaf ears, however, as the Navy and the Marine Corp wanted to get the Hornet into service as soon as possible to replace their elderly fleets of Phantoms and Corsairs.

Delivery of the F/A-18 production aircraft commenced in May 1980 when the first aircraft began arriving at the USN Operational Test and Evaluation Force. The first operational squadron to receive the Hornet was the USMC's VMFA-314 'Black Knights', which received its first aircraft in August 1982 and was declared operational on the Hornet on 7 January 1983.

The first USN squadron, VFA-113, received its first Hornets in August 1983. VFA-113 along with VFA-25 conducted the Hornets first operational cruise as part of the Carrier Air Wing (CAW) aboard the USS *Constellation* during 1985.

F/A-18D from VFA-125 over the picturesque scenery of the Sierra Nevada Mountains in May 2003. USN

The Hornets baptism of fire came in April 1986, when four squadrons, 2 USN and 2 USMC, aboard the USS *Coral Sea* took part in the raid on Libya under the code name Operation Eldorado Canyon. The F/A-18's were mainly tasked with the lethal Suppression of enemy air defences using the Texas Instruments (now Raytheon) AGM-88 HARM (High Speed Anti Radiation Missile) which was also making its operational combat debut.

The first real test for the Hornet came in the 1991 Gulf War, Operation Desert Storm, conducted between January and March. A total of 16 squadrons were involved in operations, nine USN and seven Marine Corp. Although, mainly tasked with attack roles, the aircraft were also tasked with defence suppression and CAP (Combat Air Patrols). During the campaign a pair of bomb laden Hornets claimed the types first air to air kills when they shot down a pair of Iraqi Air Force Chengdu F-7's (Chinese MiG-21 copies) then continued on to bomb the target, demonstrating the type's self-escort capability.

Following production of 371 F/A-18A and 40 F/A-18B's, the F/A-18C single seat and F/A-18D twin-seat models superseded the 'A/B' on the production line, with the first 'C' model BuNo.163427 making its maiden flight at St Louis on 3 September 1986. Improvements to the F/A-18C/D included changes to the weapons capability such as provision for the Hughes AIM-120 AMRAAM (Advanced Medium Range Air to Air Missile) active beyond visual range air to air missile, and imaging infrared AGM-65 Maverick ASM (Air to Surface Missile). Other improvements included an avionics upgrade with new AN/ALR-67 RHWR (Radar Homing and Warning Receiver). Other systems included the cancelled interchangeable reconnaissance nose for the proposed RF-18A and the cancelled AN/ALQ-165 ASPJ (Airborne self-protection Jammer), interchangeable with the AN/ALQ-126B. The 'C/D' model's also featured revisions to the mission computer, with built in test facilities, increased memory and faster processing, necessitating improvements to the Electronic Control system.

The only noticeable external feature of the F/A-18C/D over the F/A-18A/B are a five pronged antennae array for the ALR-67 RWR on the gun bay door. Also there is a small fairing on the sides of the nose and the fin trailing edge, and antennas for the ALQ-165 on the gun bay access door, nose gear door, on top of the nose and behind the canopy.

An F/A-18C prepares to launch from *the* USS *George Washington* (CVN 73) in the Atlantic Ocean in June 2000. DoD

The Martin Baker NACES ejection seat replaced the SJU-56 of the 'A/B' model. The only aerodynamic improvements are the addition of a pair of small strakes above the LERX (Leading Edge Root Extensions) designed to reduce buffet on the vertical tail fins and improve yaw control at very high angles of attack. Most early production Hornets have had the strakes retrofitted.

Following production of the first 137 F/A-18C and 31 F/A-18D's, production switched to the 'night attack' F/A-18C/D variant. These Hornets included provision for GEC Cats Eyes night vision goggles, a Raytheon AN/AAR-50 TINS, which presents its thermal picture ahead of the Kaiser AN/AVQ-28 raster HUD. They were also equipped with a Loral AN/AAS-38 targeting FLIR (Forward Looking InfraRed) pod, carried externally, and colour MFDS (Multi-Function Display Screens). A Honeywell colour digital-moving map replaced the projected moving map display; negating the need for the loading of film for projection. The first 'Night Attack' Hornet, F/A-18C BuNo.163985, was delivered to the NATC (Naval Air Training Centre) at Patuxent River, Maryland, on 1 November 1989; this being followed by the first 'Night Attack' F/A-18D, BuNo.163986, on the 14th of the month.

'Night Attack' F/A-18D's replaced the Grumman A-6E Intruder with the USMC's VMA(AW) All Weather Attack Squadrons. These aircraft have uncoupled cockpits, which usually have no control column in the rear cockpit (although one can be fitted if required). The rear cockpits had mission equipment installed, including two 12.7-cm (5in) MFDS and a moving map display operated by two side stick weapons controllers.

McDonnell Douglas and later Boeing achieved considerable success with Hornet sales to export customers. The first export customer for the Hornet was Canada, which had been targeted by Northrop as a potential launch customer for the land based F-18L, but opted instead for the F/A-18A/B. Canada eventually received 98 single-seat aircraft designated CF-18A by MDC and CF-188A by the CAF (Canadian Armed Forces), and 40 two-seat aircraft designated CF-18B by MDC and CF-188B by the CAF. The CF-188s replaced the Lockheed CF-104G Starfighter and CF-101B Voodoo in CAF service.

An F/A-18D 'Night Attack' Hornet from VMFA (AW)-533, USMC pops flares for the camera just after the end of Operation Allied Force. The squadron was deployed to Taszar Air Base in Hungary as part of MAG-31(FWD). USMC

Deliveries to Canada began in 1982 and were completed in 1988. Although virtually identical to the standard F/A-18A/B, the Canadian Hornet's were fitted with a spotlight on the port side of the nose, utilised for identifying intercepted aircraft at night. A new ILS was fitted and the aircraft were wired for the carriage of LAU-5003 rockets. Canada received 13 Loral Aeronautics NiteHawk targeting pods for its Hornet force. The pods include a FLIR, laser designator/ranger and a laser spot tracker.

Australia followed Canada, ordering 57 single-seat aircraft designated AF-18A and 18 twin-seat ATF-18A Hornets in 1981. The 75 Australian aircraft were assembled, and later produced, in Australia by ASTA. Delivered between 1985 and 1990 they replaced the Dassault Mirage III in Australian service. Surviving Australian aircraft were upgraded to F/A-18C/D standard and are wired to launch the AGM-84 Harpoon, AGM-88 HARM and Paveway II Laser Guided Bomb (LGB). Like the US and Canadian aircraft the Australian Hornets can launch the AIM-7 Sparrow. Into the 21st Century Australia equipped its Hornet's with the US AMRAAM and the European ASRAAM (Advanced Short Range Air to Air Missile) as part of its Hornet upgrade program.

The last of the three export customers to order the F/A-18A/B models was Spain with 60 single-seat EF-18A and 12 two seat EF-18Bs being ordered, deliveries commencing in 1986 and ending in 1990. Spanish EF-18As are designated C.15 and the EF-18Bs are designated CE.15 in service with the *Ejercito del Aire* (Spanish Air Force). Spanish Hornets are tasked with both air defence, suppression of enemy air defence, maritime strike and attack roles, and are equipped with the HARM and Harpoon anti-ship missile for the latter two roles respectively. Once in service the Spanish Hornets underwent some modifications from the standard F/A-18A/B and received the designations EF-18A/B+.

From early 1996, Spain began taking delivery of 24 surplus USN F/A-18A/B's ordered as interim fighters to plug the gap pending the entry into service of the EF 2000 (Eurofighter Typhoon). An option for a further six surplus USN F/A-18A's was taken up in May 1997.

The first export order for the F/A-18C/D came from Kuwait with an order for 32 F/A-18C and 8 F/A-18D'S in September 1988.

Above: An F/A-18C of VFA-87 about to take the wire while landing on the USS *Theodore Roosevelt* (CVN 71) cruising in the Atlantic Ocean in January 2003. USN

The Kuwait Hornet program was held-up by the Iraq invasion of August 1990 and the 1991 war to liberate the country. With the Gulf War over, deliveries to the Kuwait Air Force eventually commenced in February 1992 and all 40 aircraft had been delivered by September 1993. Kuwait also purchased sixteen NiteHawk targeting pods for its Hornets.

Finland selected the Hornet in 1992 with an order for 64 aircraft, the first seven F/A-18D's being built by MDC and the 57 F/A-18Cs being assembled locally by Valmet Aviation Industries in Finland. The first aircraft for Finland, an F/A-18D, serial HN-461, flew for the first time at St Louis on 21 April 1995 and was formally rolled out in June that year, deliveries commencing in September with four F/A-18D's delivered by November 1995. The first locally built F/A-18C, HN-401, made its maiden flight in the summer of 1996. The last of the 57 Finnish assembled Hornets was delivered in 2000. In Finnish service the Hornet is designated F-18C/D, these aircraft being the first export Hornets equipped with the APG-73 radar and the General Electric F404-GE-402 EPE.

Switzerland's competition for a new fighter was a long drawn out affair, the Hornet winning the competition not once, but three times. Switzerland was looking for a replacement for its fleet of Northrop F-5E", but was concerned at the lack of available thrust provided by the F404-GE-400. When the F404-GE-402 EPE became available Switzerland placed an order in October 1988. However, in 1990 the Swiss fighter competition was re-opened. Following another evaluation the Hornet was re-selected by the Swiss government. However due to the political importance of the Hornet selection the government decided to hold a national referendum and in June 1993 the population put the final seal on the order when it endorsed the Hornet selection.

The Swiss order consisted of 26 F/A-18C and eight F/A-18D's. The first F/A-18D for Switzerland's Flugwaffe (Swiss Air Force), J-5231, conducted its maiden flight on 20 January 1996, and this was followed on 8 April by F/A-18C, J-5001, both manufactured by McDonnell Douglas at St Louis. The remaining thirty-two aircraft were assembled at Emmen by the Federal Aircraft Factory, later known as the Swiss Aircraft and Systems Company (SF). The first locally built Hornet, an F/A-18D, J-5232, made its first flight from Emmen on 3 November 1996 and formally handed over to the Flugwaffe on 23 January 1997. The ALQ-165 was approved for export and selected by Finland and Switzerland for its F-18/F/A-18's.

A pair of F/A-18C let rip with salvoes of 5-in rockets. Boeing

In the early 1990's McDonnell Douglas set its sights on the Far Eastern fighter market with Malaysia emerging as the first Asian customer for the Hornet, an order being placed in June 1993. Malaysia was unique in being the only Hornet operator to order two-seat F/A-18D's only. These aircraft were to a similar standard to the USMC 'Night attack' F/A-18D. At the same time Malaysia ordered 18 MiG-29N's which were operated in the fighter role while the Hornets were operated in the strike role. The Malaysian Hornets are equipped with the APG-73 and powered by the F404-GE-402. Malaysia also ordered 4 NiteHawk targeting pods for its Hornets.

The first Hornet for Malaysia, M54-01, made its first flight on 1 February 1997 and the aircraft was handed over to the RMAF (Royal Malaysian Air Force) at St Louis on 19 March 1997.

Other potential customers would have to purchase second hand aircraft as the F/A-18C/D production line was closed in 2000.

Canadian CF-18 Hornets taxi for take-off at Aviano, Italy, during Operation Allied Force in 1999. The CF-18's are armed with AIM-9L Sidewinder air to air missiles, AGM-65 Maverick air to ground missiles and have a NiteHawk targeting pod on the port shoulder station and an AIM-7F Sparrow on the starboard shoulder station. USAF

This F/A-18A was used by NASA for the Active Aeroelastic Wing research program. The aircraft is performing a 360-degrees roll during a test flight on 7 February 2003. NASA DFRC

The USN is continually expanding the capabilities of its Hornet fleet through introduction of new software and hardware and upgrades of other systems. Although it had previously cancelled the ITT/Westinghouse ALQ-165 ASPJ on the grounds that the system had failed to meet the demanding requirements set out by the customer, it was acknowledged that the system was still more capable than the ALQ-126B used by the aircraft in the mid-1990's. This led to pressure for the release to service of some of the systems delivered before cancellation to be installed in USN/USMC Hornets operating in the Bosnia theatre and in summer 1995 the USN installed ALQ-165 systems on 12 F/A-18's operating over Bosnia. These systems had been in storage since 1992. The temporary installation was implemented to counter Serbian SA-6 SAM (Surface to Air Missiles).

The USN had plans for a suppression of enemy air defences capability similar to that achieved for the Block 50/52 F-16C/D for its F/A-18C/D's. Loral tested a pylon mounted precision emitter-location system on an USN F/A-18 in 1993, and Litton was developing an advanced digital receiver which would fit inside the ALR-67 RWR, Providing a precision direction-finding and identification capability using the existing antennae. Flight testing in an F/A-18 was conducted from 1996, but the program was dropped.

As the Super Hornet was on the cusp of entering service a number of upgrades were being introduced for the first generation Hornet. Including installation of Litton LN-100G integrated global-positioning/inertial navigation system, which combines the LN-100 laser gyro/INS with a Rockwell-Collins GPS-receiver module. Other improvements to the radar will continue as the systems potential is further developed. Some F/A-18E/F Super Hornet crew station enhancements may also filter through to the Hornet fleet.

An F/A-18C, armed with AMRAAM, Sidewinder and HARM missiles, prepares to launch. DoD

In December 1998, USN F/A-18C/D's operating from the aircraft carrier USS *Enterprise* participated in the four day Operation Desert Fox air campaign against Iraq. USN and USMC Hornets routinely flew patrols in support of Operation Southern Watch in the Gulf. In the two and a half years following Desert Fox, American and British aircraft launched a large number of strikes against Iraqi targets. F/A-18C/D's have been involved in some of these operations, one of which saw the operational debut of the Raytheon AGM-154 JSOW (Joint Stand-Off Weapon) in January 1999. The patrols over Iraq were conducted by the US and UK as a unilateral operation, the attacks on Iraq resulting in condemnation all across the globe.

In March 1999, NATO launched operation Allied Force, an air campaign against Serbia to force its withdrawal from Kosovo. Hornets from the US, Spain and Canada conducted a large number of sorties during the campaign. Canada provided 24 CF-18As, which flew 650 sorties. Spain provided 6 Hornets and 36 F/A-18C/D's operated from the US carrier in the Adriatic. From late May 1999 the USMC MAG 31FWD deployed 24 F/A-18D's to Hungary and these aircraft flew a total 220 sorties, including 22 sorties with two aircraft equipped with the ATARS (Advanced Tactical Airborne Reconnaissance System) reconnaissance system, which was making its operational debut.

From October 2001 US Hornets flew operations over Afghanistan and the tempo of operations over Iraq increased in March 2003 when the US, UK and Australia invaded that country.

The F/A-18 replaced the F-4 Phantom II and A-7 Corsair II in USN service, and the 'Night Attack' F/A-18D replaced the A-6E in USMC service. The versatility of the aircraft allowed Hornet to replace some A-6E Intruder and F-14 Tomcat squadrons in the USN, with the Tomcat taking on some of the Intruders strike roles following the withdrawal of the A-6 in 1996.

With tens of USN and USMC squadrons along with other support units remaining established the first generation Hornet still has a long service life ahead of it. With the benefit of life extension and system upgrades it will serve alongside the larger F/A-18E/F Super Hornet on the USN carrier decks through the second decade of this Century.

Chapter 2

SUPER HORNET GENESIS

In the late 1980's the USN was looking forward to production of the Advanced A-6F variant of the Intruder. The prototype, BuNo.162183, made its first flight from Grumman's Long Island facility on 26 August 1987. Grumman History Centre

In the early 1980s USN planners were looking for a suitable replacement for the services premier strike aircraft, the Grumman A-6 Intruder, which had made its first flight in prototype A2F-1 form as far back as 19 April 1960, and had been in operational service since February 1963. While the A-6E variant equipping squadrons in the 1980's was still a capable strike platform, having undergone numerous upgrades since the days of the A-6A, the basic design was getting somewhat long in the tooth and was becoming increasingly vulnerable to modern surface to air threats. In addition, maintenance of the ageing airframes and engines was becoming more of a problem with each passing year.

At this time USAF research and development funding was paying dividends with major breakthroughs in 'stealth' technology for its future combat aircraft designs. While ultimately the USN wanted to get into the 'stealth' aircraft business its urgent requirement for a stopgap replacement for at least a part of its A-6E fleet required a more readily available solution.

The A-6 had proved an outstanding success in service; having been combat proven in the skies over Vietnam, therefore, the obvious answer to replace the A-6 was a new A-6 with new engines and modern avionics and weapons systems. While the USN pressed on with plans for an advanced 'stealthy' strike aircraft under its ATA (Advanced Tactical Aircraft) program it was decided that the service should procure a number of new build A-6F Intruder II's pending the availability of the ATA in the mid to late 1990s.

The A-6F was originally known as the A-6E upgrade, a development contract being awarded to Grumman in July 1984. Although retaining the familiar airframe of the A-6E, the A-6F was virtually a new aircraft, with new radar, which would significantly enhance the aircraft capability, digitised avionics and new engines. A pair of smokeless General Electric 45-kN (10,800-lb) non-afterburning F404-GE-400D turbofan engines replaced the J52 turbojets of the A-6E. General Electric had been conducting growth studies of the F404 since 1983.

The A-6F prototype is towed from the assembly building to the paint shop at Bethpage. Grumman History Centre

The Norden APQ-173 synthetic aperture radar (some documentation suggests that the radar never officially received this designation) not only further enhanced the A-6F air to surface potential, but introduced new air to air modes, including AIM-120 AMRAAM capability. Although the Intruder could never be considered a fighter, the AMRAAM capability bestowed upon it the capability to engage hostile fighters in beyond visual range combat, in effect giving the Intruder II a self-escort capability not to dissimilar to that enjoyed by the USAF McDonnell Douglas (now Boeing) F-15E Eagle strike aircraft. According to Norden the new radar would "…increase the range at which Intruder crews can detect, identify and track land and sea targets, and it will permit the accurate delivery of air to ground ordnance and air to air missiles."

The A-6F cockpit was completely modernised with a new digital instrument panel and five MFDS (Multi-Function Displays Screens) driven by an AYX-14 tactical computer.

The A-6F prototype, BuNo.162183, conducted its maiden flight from Grumman's Bethpage Facility on Long Island on 26 August 1987. With the aircraft urgently required to replace those A-6E's in most need of retirement, development work was conducted at a quick pace. At the same time Grumman was involved in the USN F-14D Tomcat program, therefore, a joint A-6F/F-14D development office was established at the NATC (Naval Air Training Centre), Patuxent River, Maryland, with service deliveries of both aircraft expected to commence in the early 1990's. In 1986, it was reported that the USN would receive 120 new A-6F's and the USMC would receive 30, all to be delivered by 1995.

A further four A-6F development aircraft were built. Of these BuNos.162184 and 162185 joined the flight test program. The two remaining aircraft, BuNos.162186 and 162187, were never flown; being put into storage at Bethpage when the program was abruptly cancelled in 1988 when the Pentagon decided that the USN should soldier on with the A-6E, which would receive some improvements, until the ATA entered service in the mid-1990's.

Following cancellation of the A-6F, Grumman proposed a more modest Intruder update known as the A-6G, which would have incorporated most of the systems planned for the A-6F, although it would have retained the General Electric J52-P-409 turbojet engines of the A-6E. The third prototype A-6F, BuNo162185, became the DSD (Digital Systems Development) aircraft, testing the various systems for the A-6G. In reality the A-6G was 'doomed' from the start as the USN was committed to procuring a 'stealthy' replacement for the Intruder through the ATA program and had no available funding for new Intruder variants.

The A-6DSD was a more modest update for the Intruder, which emerged following the cancellation of the A-6F program. Grumman History Centre

The Advanced Tactical Aircraft program was revealed in 1985 as a 'stealthy' subsonic all weather deep penetration strike aircraft. Although revealed in 1985, the program had been underway for some time prior to this to meet a USN requirement for a stealthy replacement for the A-6 Intruder from the mid-1990's. As the USN had diverted little funds to the development of 'stealth' technology the ATA drew on much of the technology developed with USAF funding. At the same time the USAF was pursuing the ATF (Advanced Tactical Fighter) program (eventually won by the Lockheed/Boeing F-22 Raptor). In April 1986, a MoU (Memorandum of Understanding) was signed between the USAF and the USN under which the former would consider the ATA as a potential replacement for it General Dynamics F-111 and later F-15E strike aircraft. It was projected at this time that the USAF could expect delivery of its first ATA in 1998.

Both services embarked on a joint program to develop a new powerplant that could be suitable for both the ATA and the ATF under the JAFE (Joint Advanced Fighter Engine) program that produced the rival Pratt & Whitney F119 and General Electric F120 engines for the ATF competition. The USN eventually withdrew from the JAFE program when it became clear that the ATF engines would not be suitable for integration into the ATA.

When the USN issued a request for proposals for its ATA requirement only two teams responded. General Dynamics was teamed with McDonnell Douglas and Northrop teamed with Grumman and LTV. The Northrop proposal for the ATA was said to have been a flying wing described as a "scaled down Northrop B-2" and this was seen as the favourite to win the contract. The other major manufactures Lockheed, Boeing and Rockwell appear not to have submitted any proposals. On 20 December 1987 the Northrop/Grumman/LTV team declined to submit 'best and final' bids for the ATA and four days later, the 24th, the General Dynamics/McDonnell Douglas team was declared the winner of the competition with an initial $241,000.00 contract being awarded. General Dynamics was the prime contractor with McDonnell Douglas the principal sub-contractor.

The General Dynamics/McDonnell Douglas ATA, which was designated A-12, was designed as an extremely 'stealth' driven flying wing. It was to be a two-seat strike aircraft capable of carrying a large payload in an internal weapons bay, with a combat radius of 1850-km (1,000-nm) without in-flight refuelling.

The General Dynamics/McDonnell Douglas A-12 Avenger II was designed as an extremely stealth oriented strike platform. The program was extremely challenging, both technically and politically, and it was a combination of the two that eventually led to its demise in 1991. DoD

As the USN had pulled out of the JAFE program it decided to power the A-12 with a pair of uprated non-afterburning derivatives of the General Electric F404 turbofan which powered the F/A-18A/B/C/D Hornet. This powerplant was originally known as the F404/F5D2, but later matured into the F412-GE-400. To keep development and thus unit costs to a minimum the A-12 was to be a subsonic aircraft with no real STOL (short take-off and landing) capability. The strike mission required that the aircraft be capable of penetrating enemy defences at ultra low level in all weather and in a dense ECCM (Electronic Counter Counter Measures) environment. Early in the program, take-off weight was estimated at around 25000-kg (55,000-lb), although as the program developed weight grew to the point where the contractors were experiencing difficulty in keeping within the specification weight limit of 60,000-lb.

The A-12 ATA was a more stealth driven design than the ATF competitors, the YF-22 and the YF-23, incorporating more RAM (Radar Absorbent Material) in its construction. The design was so stealth driven that some in the program were predicting that it would not require an active radar jammer as existing and projected hostile radar would simply not be capable of detecting the aircraft.

The A-12's radar, developed by Westinghouse, was to have incorporated ISA (Inverse Synthetic Array) technology which was also planned for the Norden Systems APQ-173 radar developed for the A-6F Intruder II. The resolution was expected to be good enough for the class of a ship to be determined at a range of 150-km (90 miles). Air to air modes for the radar would allow the use of the AIM-120 AMRAAM beyond visual range air to air missile. This would have bestowed a true self escort capability upon the A-12. Westinghouse was also developing a navigation and targeting IR Infrared Sensor) and Litton Amecon was developing the ESM (Electronic Sensor Measures) suite.

In the mid-1980's the unit fly-away cost of an A-12 was estimated at $40 million, although even at this time the predictions were for a much more expensive unit cost and this had grown to $80-$96 million flyaway unit cost by 1989.

Had fortune shone more brightly on the troubled A-12 it was to have commenced replacing the A-6E fleet from the mid-to-late 1990's with at least 450 aircraft expected to have been purchased for the USN, while a further 60 would have went to the USMC. If the A-12 proved to be too expensive for the Marine Corp then the F/A-18D 'Plus' would be purchased as an A-6E replacement.

Following the cancellation of the A-6F Intruder II in 1988, the ATA program took on even greater urgency as maintenance was becoming an ever increasing problem for the elderly A-6E airframes and systems. ATA production totals were also increased to an estimated 620 units, and in spring 1988 the US DoD approved plans for assembly of the A-12 at McDonnell Douglas's facility - Air Force Plant 3 at Tulsa International Airport, Oklahoma. This site, which was government owned, was said to be conveniently located for both contractors.

The first A-12 prototype, BuNo.164519, eventually named Avenger II, was initially expected to make its first flight in 1990 and some eight aircraft were to have been completed by the end of the year. Following the revelation of program delays the first flight was grudgingly re-scheduled for mid-1991 and then again for March 1992, the design team claiming the slip was due to "complexity and unanticipated delays in the tooling required for the aircraft."

In early 1990, the, then US Defence Secretary, Dick Cheney was "not happy" with the delays in the A-12 program, and with the fact that these problems had been omitted from the Pentagons MAR (Major Aircraft Review) conducted in the spring of 1990.

Among the main iterations of the Grumman (now Northrop Grumman) F-14 Tomcat put forward as candidates for a new fleet strike fighter was the Tomcat 21 seen in model form above. Grumman History Centre

On 11 June 1990, Cheney summoned the then chairman of General Dynamics, Stanley Pace and MDC's John F McDonnell for an explanation as to why the A-12 delays had escaped the MAR. Following the meeting Cheney addressed a news conference saying "I was not happy with the A-12." He also claimed that the program had "high priority." USN sources claimed that the contractors were experiencing difficulty in building the all-composite A-12 to the required specification weights which set out a loaded weight of 60,000-lb, slightly more than the A-6E which it was to replace.

Adding further to the crisis that was beginning to grip the future of US carrier aviation at the end of December 1990, the defence secretary signed a program decision memorandum which in effect denied the funding of any more new production F-14D Tomcat fighters. In addition, the memorandum also denied funding for increased upgrading of F-14A's to F-14D standard. USN supporters of the Tomcat had hoped to upgrade the aircraft further, giving it a strike role, which would at least partly compensate for the pending withdrawal of the A-6 fleet. However, Cheney announced that he was instead calling for the allocation of some $3.5 billion in funding to develop an upgraded F/A-18 Hornet, which would eventually emerge as the F/A-18E/F Super Hornet. This program was seen as a fall back against failure of the A-12, which was facing an increasingly uncertain future.

This decision came in the same month that Secretary of the USN, H. Lawrence Garret, requested that the F-14 be restored to full production, stating that the F-14 could be given the added strike role. He went on to claim that it would be better for the USN to rely on the proven Tomcat for the air to air role as opposed to procurement of the more expensive navalised variant of the ATF then being proposed as the USN's future fleet air defence fighter, with up to 550 aircraft being envisaged. He proposed building 12, 24 and 24 Tomcats in FY's 92, 93 and 94 respectively for the same cost as re-manufacturing F-14A's into F-14D's at a rate of 18, 36, and 36 in the same time period.

Adding further to the troubles facing USN tactical aviation in the early 1990's was the decision to deny funding for any more new F-14D Tomcats or further upgrades of the F-14A to F-14D. DoD

He also proposed that the USN purchase 132 new F-14D's between FY 1992 and 1997. At the same time he argued for production of a longer ranged Hornet beginning in FY 1995.

The axe finally fell on the troubled A-12 program when Cheney announced its cancellation on 7 January 1991, citing mismanagement and the inability of the contractors to design, develop, fabricate, assemble and test the aircraft within the contract schedule, and to deliver to the USN an aircraft that met the contract requirements. Immediately following the A-12 cancellation most of the major aircraft companies were knocking on the Pentagons door in desperate attempts to sell variants of existing hardware to replace the A-12 program. Long before the demise of the A-12, these same companies had continued wok on advanced developments of their existing fighters in case of either delay or cancellation of the ATA program. As far back as July 1987, Casper Weinberger, then US Secretary of Defence, told the USN and USAF to look at upgrades of their respective fleets of F/A-18 Hornets, F-15 Eagle and General Dynamics F-16 Fighting Falcons in case of delays, cuts, or cancellation to the A-12 and ATF programs. To this end McDonnell Douglas had been working on an advanced Hornet variant designated Hornet 2000 and had looked at a number of options including variants fitted with a dorsal fuel tank and a completely redesigned variant featuring an arrow shaped wing with canard foreplanes. The Hornet 2000 program was axed in 1988, although MDC continued its studies on a private basis.

In January 1991, following the demise of the A-12, the USN was facing a tactical combat aircraft crisis. With production of the A-6 terminated and Grumman F-14 production coming to an end, the only tactical fighter program left for the USN was the F/A-18, which had neither the range nor load carrying capability of either the A-6 or F-14. Therefore, it was decided that the search for an advanced strike aircraft would go on under the A-X program, but as this was unlikely to be available before 2005/6, by which time the much of the USN's ageing fleet of F-14, F/A-18 and A-6's would be beyond their life expectancy, an interim fighter would have to be procured as a stop-gap measure to ensure the combat efficiency of US Naval air power. MDC proposed its study of an upgraded Hornet, which it was revealed, would be a stretched and improved variant of the Hornet 2000. In the spring of 1991, the first basic impressions of the new Hornet variant, already dubbed F/A-18E/F, appeared in the press.

By the mid-1990's the USN was increasingly relying on the F/A-18C/D for the strike fighter roles, exacerbated with the retirement of the Grumman A-6E Intruder in 1996. However, the F/A-18C/D was wanting in range and bring-back capability and could not fill the void that was being left by the retirement of the A-6E Intruder. DoD

MDC received a $25m engineering study contract for its Hornet proposal, which ran until January 1992. Early details of the F/A-18E/F emerged showing an aircraft that had been radically altered in size compared with the original Hornet. The new F/A-18E would have its maximum take-off weight increased by 5622-kg (11,600-lb) and both E and F models would have a 0.86-m (21-ft 10-in) fuselage plug. The scaled up wing would be 25% larger with an additional 9.29-m2 (100 sq. ft) of wing area and an additional 1.30 m (4 ft 3.5 in) span.

As the new fighter would be much larger and heavier than the existing F/A-18C/D a more powerful powerplant was required, General Electric, Pratt & Whitney and Allison Engines all submitting bids; General Electric being selected to an improved variant of the F404 installed in F/A-18A/B/C/D Hornets. The new engine, designated F414, would be rated at around 9071-kg to 9978-kg (20,000-lb to 22,000-lb) and would use technology developed for the non-afterburning F412 powerplant of the cancelled A-12 leading to early reports suggesting that the new F414 would be non-afterburning vastly reducing the aircraft's infrared signature, although these reports proved fallacious and the F414 indeed featured afterburning, providing up to 35% more thrust over the F404 which compensated for the roughly 24.5% increase in empty weight and slightly over 15% increase in MTOW over the F/A-18C/D.

The increased power level also allowed the designers to address one of the main criticisms of the F/A-18C/D, that of bring-back fuel/payload. The larger internal volume allowed an extra 2997-kg (4,620-lb) of internal fuel to be carried compared with the F/A-18C/D which helped to address the range deficiency of the Hornet. In addition, the new fighter could carry 4926 kg (10,860-lb) of external fuel compared with the 3053-kg (6,732-lb) carried by the 'C/D'. MDC claimed that the larger fuel volume would give the F/A-18E/F a range increase of some 40% compared with the F/A-18C/D, although this figure was later reduced to 38%.

The Boeing A-X jet –Effects model undergoing testing in the 16 foot transonic wind-tunnel at the NASA Langley Research Centre. NASA LaRC

Following the cancellation of the A/F-X, Lockheed Martin revived proposals for a naval variant of the F-117 Nighthawk as an A-6E replacement. This naval variant of the 'Black Jet' would have been designated A/F-117X. Lockheed Martin

In 1991, MDC claimed that the new F/A-18E/F would have a combat radius of 400-nm while carrying four MK 83, 227-kg (500-lb) bombs, two AIM-9M Sidewinders, two 150-kg (330-lb) external tanks and mission sensors such as pod a mounted FLIR. While this fell far short of the range of the A-6E it would be a great improvement over the F/A-18C/D, which with the same load could operate to a radius of only 290-nm. On a fleet air defence mission while carrying four AIM-120 AMRAAM's, two Sidewinders and two external fuel tanks at a range of 400-nm the F/A-18E/F could loiter on Combat Air Patrol (CAP) for 71 minutes, while the Grumman F-14D Tomcat fleet air defence fighter could loiter for only 58 minutes.

Throughout 1991, the design was changed and refined, and in the autumn of 1991 it was revealed that the engine intakes had been completely redesigned out of all recognition with first generation Hornets. The 'D' shaped intake of the original Hornet was replaced by a trapezoidal configuration allowing 18% more air to the more powerful engines. The sharply raked intakes would also allow better high-speed performance and it was hoped that they would contribute to reducing the aircraft's radar signature.

Another company that hoped to capitalise on the cancellation of the A-12 was Grumman, which had conducted studies on a number of advanced Tomcat variants. Grumman was not slow in putting these forward as alternatives to the proposed F/A-18E/F. The first of the Tomcat variants offered as an alternative to the F/A-18E/F was the F-14 'Quickstrike' which had minimum changes from the F-14D to minimise development costs. The 'Quickstrike' would have additional air to surface modes for its Westinghouse AN/APG-71 radar, including Synthetic Aperture and Doppler-beam sharpening for ground mapping, similar to the APG-70 radar fitted to the F-15E Eagle. A forward-looking infrared (FLIR), probably the LANTIRN (Low Altitude Navigation and Targeting InfraRed for Night) navigation and targeting system would also have been incorporated. The four fuselage hardpoints had five sub-stations each, enhancing offensive capability. The wing pylons retained the standard two sub-stations. The cockpit would be further modernised by including a new or improved HUD Heads-Up Display), FLIR, MMD (Moving Map Display) and colour display screens, and would be fully night vision capable. Precision guided munitions capability were a high priority and software changes would allow compatibility with the AGM-88 HARM, AGM-65 Maverick, LGB's, AGM-84E SLAM and AGM-84 Harpoon missiles.

The Super Tomcat 21 was proposed as a more advanced update of the 'Quickstrike', as a low cost alternative to the expensive and ultimately unaffordable Naval ATF. Grumman claimed that the Super Tomcat 21 would offer 90% of the ATF capability at 60% of the cost. It would have incorporated advanced avionics, reduced signature and improved GE-F110-GE-129 engines, which would enable it to supercruise (sustain supersonic cruising speed without the use of afterburner). Thrust-vectoring control, which would both improve manoeuvrability and take-off performance, was another option to be considered. Although the main differences over existing Tomcats would be internal, the Super Tomcat 21 would have enlarged tailplanes, increased-lift slotted flaps, extended chord slotted flaps allowing nil-wind carrier take-off at higher weights and new extended wing gloves housing additional internal fuel. Among the new advanced avionics systems would be a HMSS (Helmet Mounted Sighting System), FLIR and new radar with twice the power of the AN/APG-71 fitted in the F-14D.

A more radical variant of the Super Tomcat 21 known as the Attack Super Tomcat 21 was proposed as an A-6E replacement. This variant would have had thicker outer wing panels that would have housed additional fuel, which together with the provision for larger external fuel tanks would have seen a significant range increase. Refinements to the high lift system would have given a 15-Knot (27-km/h; 18-mph) reduction in approach speed. At the heart of the Attack Super Tomcat 21's capabilities would be the Norden attack radar developed for the cancelled A-12.

A further proposed upgrade of the Tomcat as an ATF alternative was the ASF-14, which would have had the powerplant and systems of the ATF in a refined Tomcat airframe.

The USN upgraded a number of F-14 Tomcats for the strike role as a stop-gap measure to partially replace the capability lost with the retirement of the A-6E fleet. Here an F-14 is seen releasing a laser-guided- bomb. The F-14 proved a success in the strike role, but the fleet was progressively withdrawn until final retirement in 2006. DoD

In March 1991, the USN prepared a briefing for Congress outlining the praises of the F/A-18, also claiming its ability to take over the air superiority role from the F-14 Tomcat as an alternative to procurement of the Naval ATF. The document also outlined the Hornets combat record in operation Desert Storm, in which campaign the USN and USMC deployed 190 Hornets in theatre, including 106 on aircraft carriers and 84 land based Marine Corp aircraft. Of this total only three aircraft were lost to enemy action and non-combat related accidents. A further three aircraft were hit by infrared guided surface to air missiles, but managed to return to their carriers where they were repaired and returned to service. The USMC Hornets flew between 120 and 220 sorties per day during the course of the campaign.

During February 1991, 12 USMC F/A-18D 'Night Attack' Hornets accumulated 1,427 flight hours equating to an average of 118.9 hours per aircraft with no losses, and at the end of the month all twelve aircraft were serviceable and ready for operations. Surpassing this record was the two Hornet squadrons of the USS *Saratoga*, CV-60, with

2,313 flight hours accumulated in February for an average of 128.5 hours per aircraft. The briefing also outlined the Hornets multi-role versatility by the fact that Hornets flew six different missions during the course of the campaign: fleet air defence, suppression of enemy air defence, interdiction, close air support, self escort and offensive and defensive counter air.

Following a meeting of the defence acquisition board on 5 May 1992 the DoD gave the go-ahead for the F/A-18E/F program, and an EMD (Engineering & Manufacturing Development) contract valued at $4.88 billion was awarded on 1 June that year. The EMD was to run for seven and a half years and involved the building of five single-seat F/A-18E development aircraft, three (later reduced to two) two-seat F/A-18F's and three static test airframes for ground based structural testing. The procurement program for 1,000 aircraft was through 2014/15.

The program continued to come under criticisms as providing only marginal improvements over the 'C/D' Hornet at such a large cost. Some believed the F/A-18E/F was robbing the USN of funding for the true A-12 replacement, the A-X., which was then being studied as a low-observable complement to the F/A-18E/F and as such was seen as the true A-6 replacement. In parallel the USAF had embarked on the MRF (Multi-Role Fighter) program in search of a replacement for its large fleet of F-16 and Fairchild A-10 Thunderbolt II tactical fighters and ground attack aircraft.

In mid-1992, the HASC (House Armed Services Committee) FY93 budget proposed acceleration of the A-X program, requiring that existing sub-systems such as avionics and engines developed for other aircraft be used, and that two competitive prototypes be built by rival teams before selection of a winning design. This was to be at the expense of the F/A-18E/F program resulting in the USN request for $1.1b in funding for the latter being cut by $535m.

The A-X study later broadened into the A/F-X as a multi-role strike fighter replacement for not only the A-6, but also the USAF's General Dynamics F-111E/F, MDC F-15E Eagle and Lockheed F-117A Nighthawk strike aircraft. All the usual suspects were involved in studies for the A/F-X. The General Dynamics/McDonnell Douglas team had planned to bid a variant of the cancelled A-12 Avenger II to meet the A/F-X requirement. However, following Lockheed's acquisition of General Dynamics in 1992/3, the company disbanded the General Dynamics design team working on the A/F-X as Lockheed was designing competing AF/X designs including a variant of the winner of the USAF ATF contest, the Lockheed/Boeing F-22. Lockheed was also proposing a variant of the F-16 designated F-16X to meet the USAF MRF requirement, claiming that the F-16X, which would feature a new wing based on that of the F-22 and no horizontal tail, would have twice the range of the F/A-18E/F at only two thirds of the cost.

In August 1993, the Pentagon's Bottom-up review of defence recommended that the USN/USAF A/F-X and the USAF's MRF be cancelled, while at the same time confirming early retirement plans for the A-6E by the year 2000. On the positive side it recommended continuation of the F/A-18E/F for the USN and the F-22 for the USAF. The review also nominated the F/A-18E/F as a replacement for the F-16 and A-10A and also set the future carrier fleet at 11 (later reinstated to 12) active vessels, one of which would be in reserve with ten active and one reserve air wings. In addition to continuation of the F/A-18E/F and F-22 programs, the review recommended that both services, combined with the USMC, began planning for a future common strike fighter with an in service date of around 2012. This latter program would eventually result in the JAST (Joint Advanced Strike Technology) and later JSF (Joint Strike Fighter), Boeing X-32 and Lockheed Martin/Northrop Grumman/British Aerospace (now BAE Systems) X-35 demonstrator programs.

Following cancellation of the A/F-X most of the USN opponents to the F/A-18E/F came into line, thankful now for whatever they could get, while at the same time the USAF vehemently rejected any notion of the F/A-18E/F being adopted as an F-16 replacement. With the A/F-X now consigned to oblivion like the A-12 before it, Lockheed revived its proposal for a carrier-based variant of the F-117 for the USN as an A-6E replacement. The original proposal, designated F-117N (N for naval), would have retained the same basic design of the USAF F-117A, although stronger materials would have been added to allow the aircraft to be operated in the demanding carrier operational environment. An off-the-shelf ACLS (Automatic Carrier Landing System) would have been included. Following its 1992 decision to develop the F/A-18E/F as its future strike fighter the USN requested Lockheed to stop pushing the unwanted 'Black Jet'. Lockheed. However, pretty much chose to ignore these pleas and continued with development of a variant of the F-117 more suited to operations from an aircraft carrier deck.

Lockheed completely redesigned the F-117 for the naval role and began proposing a new variant designated A/F-117X. This new variant would have a similar maximum take-off weight to the proposed F-117Bs maximum take-off weight of 33203-kg (73,200-lb). It would also have a larger payload and be powered by the F414 powerplant being developed for the F/A-18E/F, which was also proposed for the F-117B being offered to the USAF. The A/F-117X would have been fitted with the F-14 Tomcats landing gear and the fuselage would have been strengthened to take the stress of carrier operations. The most obvious external differences would be the new trapezoidal horizontal tail, reworked exhaust area and a new bubble cockpit canopy based on the canopy designed for the F-22. For carrier operations an arrestor hook would have been fitted and the aircraft would have featured folding wings. Lockheed claimed an AIM-120 AMRAAM and AIM-9X Sidewinder capability for the A/F-117X which was to be equipped with an unspecified radar. While the A/F-117X would undoubtedly have been an excellent strike platform it had little support in the Pentagon and even less support in the USN and was, therefore, ultimately doomed; joining the A-12, A-X, A/F-X and various advanced Tomcat variants in the league of USN 'could have beans.'

Meanwhile development of the F/A-18E/F continued to gather pace. During the 20,000-hour wind-tunnel program, which included MDC testing a 5% scale model of the F/A-18E/F in Boeings 2.4-m x 3.6-m wind-tunnel near Seattle, Washington, it was found that the LERX's were inadequate. This reduced manoeuvrability at high angles of attack and would need to be substantially increased in area. As originally proposed in 1991 the F/A-18E/F wing area had been increased from the 5.1 m2 (54.9 sq.-ft) of the F/A-18C/D to 5.8-m2 (62.4-sq-ft). It would now be necessary to increase it further to 7.0-m2 (75.3-sq-ft), an increase of just over 27% over that of the F/A-18C/D. This new feature was accepted by the design team and by early 1993 had been incorporated into the design, wind-tunnel tests confirming the suitability of the larger LERX's.

The 20,000-hour wind-tunnel program was successfully completed in 1994, although further wind tunnel testing was naturally carried out periodically since then.

As with all earlier variants of the Hornet, MDC was the prime contractor with Northrop (later Northrop Grumman) as the principal sub-contractor. The first fabrication work on the first prototype, F/A-18E1, BuNo.165164, began at St Louis on 25 May 1994. It was decided that the F/A-18E/F would be built on a new production line, which was officially opened on 23 September 1994 in a ceremony at St Louis when workers placed two nose landing gear braces onto the forward fuselage and nose of F/A18E1 onto its tooling, officially opening the F/A18E/F production line. Economies were achieved in the production of the F/A-18E/F due to the fact that the new variant had 33% fewer parts that the F/A-18C/D and the man-hours for fabrication and aircraft assembly was around 12% under budget for the prototypes.

The manufacturer and its partners made use of facilities such as those provided by NASA. Here a 15% model of the F/A-18E Super Hornet is undergoing power-effects testing in a wind tunnel at NASA Langley Research Centre. NASA LaRC

Early 1995 saw the joining of the forward fuselage to the Northrop Grumman built rear fuselage of F/A-18E1 by a computer controlled laser-guided alignment system, the first time that this precise method had been used. May 1995 also saw the delivery of the first 'flight ready' General Electric F414 turbofan engine. The prototype was completed in late summer 1995, and was rolled-out at St Louis on 18 September that year at which time the Chief of Naval Operations, Admiral Jeremy Boorda, officially named the aircraft 'Super Hornet'.

Chapter 3

SUPER HORNET DESCRIBED

A production F/A-18F from VFA-122 at NAS Lemoore, over the mountains of Southern California. Boeing

The Boeing F/A-18E/F is a fundamentally redesigned, stretched outgrowth of the F/A-18C/D Hornet. The new aircraft has a 2 ft 10 in fuselage plug inserted, which increases overall length to 18.2 m (60.3 ft) compared with the 17.07 m (56 ft) of the F/A-18C. The increased span wings measure 12.76 m (41 ft. 10.75 in) compared with 11.43 m (37 ft. 6 in) on the 'C/D' and the aircraft stands at a height of 4.8 m (16 ft) compared with the 4.66 m (15 ft 3.5 in) of the 'C/D'. Wing area, at 46.45 sq. m (500.00 sq. ft.), is increased by 25% from the 37.16 sq. m (400.00 sq. ft.) on the 'C/D'. As well as increasing the wing size by 25%, the wing root has been deepened by 2.5 cm (1 in). Although it is superficially the same as the F/A-18C wing it has no twist or camber; is new in the detail of its structure and is stressed to take the increased weights of the larger aircraft. The larger wings also featured an additional two stores stations, No 2 and No 10, located about two-thirds of span outboard of the No.3 and No.9 stations. The two additional stations are stressed for the carriage of loads up to 520-kg (1,146-lb).

The LERXs (Leading-Edge Root Extensions) have been increased in area from 5.1 sq. m (54.9 sq. ft) on the F/A-18C/D to 7.0 sq. m (75.3 sq. ft) on the F/A-18E/F. The larger LERXs went some way to restoring the manoeuvrability enjoyed by the first generation Hornet at 30-35 degrees AoA (Angle of Attack).

An F/A-18F from VFA-122 begins taxing for take off at the start of its display at Le Bourget on 16 June 2001. H Harkins

Other changes to improve the aircraft's high AoA handling include the addition of spoilers on the LERXs, which act like foreplanes to increase nose down control, and vents in the wing roots, which open to improve airflow over the fins. These changes were incorporated to prevent "falling leaf" departures experienced with first generation Hornets, caused by a lack-of nose down control at aft centre-off-gravity positions.

The horizontal fins, at 5.6 sq. m (60-sq. ft.), are 15% larger in area over those of the F/A-18C/D, and these are attached to the larger fuselage by a new manufacturing method. The rudders, which are 54% larger in area over those of the F/A-18C/D, can be deflected to an angle of 40°, 10° more than the first-generation Hornet. The airbrake found on the first generation Hornet has been deleted.

Apart from the aircraft's increased size, the most distinctive feature was the new sharply raked rectangular section engine air intakes, in contrast to the 'D' shaped intakes of the first generation Hornet. Less obvious, the F/A-18E/F has a modified, strengthened, undercarriage, allowing a MTOW (Maximum Take-Off weight) of 29937 kg (66,000-lb) compared with the 23541 kg (51,900-lb) MTOW of the F/A-18C/D. Empty weight of the F/A-18E/F is 13864 kg (30,564-lb).

The F/A-18E/F has 30% fewer parts than the 'C/D' extensive use of composite materials being made in its construction. The aluminium content is reduced from the 50% on the 'C/D' to 29% by weight, by carbon epoxy panels on the wing, centre and rear fuselage and tail surfaces, reducing weight.

F/A-18E5, foreground, and F/A-18F2, background, in formation over China Lake in 1998. While the two-seat F model was originally intended for the conversion training role it was further developed into a family of variants such as the EA-18 and the 'missionized' variant of the F/A-18F. NAWC-WD

The General Electric F414-GE-400 afterburning turbofan engine delivers around 22,000-lb of thrust in full afterburner. H Harkins

A pair of General Electric F414-GE-400 turbofan engines, each rated at 97.8-kN (22,000-lb) with afterburner, powers the Super Hornet. As previously recounted this engine was developed from the F412 engine developed for the A-12, which was itself, a development of the F404 powering first generation Hornets.

Early developments included testing various improved fans, cores, and combustors and some of this technology was utilised in the development of the F412-GE-400, which was a medium-bypass non-afterburning turbofan. The F412 had an improved core known as Core II, running at temperatures 111K hotter than the standard core used in the F404, while at the same time handling up to 5% more airflow. In concert General Electric conducted studies of afterburning engines using the same Core II as used in the F412-GE-400. This latter program drew on technology developed for the companies YF120 variable cycle turbofan then being developed as a contender to power the USAF ATF. Following four years of full-scale development the F412 was cancelled along with the A-12 in January 1991.

The F414's higher performance was obtained by incorporating several advanced technologies already proven on General Electric's family of military, and commercial engines. With details emerging of a much larger Hornet variant, General Electric was well advanced with an improved F404 powerplant known as the F404 Growth II Plus. This engine, while being derived from the basic F404, used the core of the F412 and incorporated an advanced low-pressure system developed from technology developed for the YF120.

An overview of key F414 components reflects the risk-reduction philosophy inherent in General Electric development programs: The F414 fan provides a 16 percent increase in airflow over the F404 fan, with bird-strike tolerant characteristics adapted from the F404/RM12 developed for the Swedish Saab JAS 39 Gripen and F412 fans. The first stage has removable blades; a tandem bladed disk (blisk) design is used in the second and third stages for reduced weight and cost, improved performance and ease of maintenance.

Mock-up F414 alongside an F/A-18F at the Paris Air Show in Le Bourget, in June 2001, showing the first stage removable blades. The more powerful F414 fan provides a 16% increase in airflow over the F404. Hugh Harkins

The F414 core is based on the F412 design, which originated in the GE23A demonstrator engine. The high-pressure compressors first three stages feature a blisk design. The high-pressure turbine is based on the F412 turbine design. The improved durability, cooling and maintainability features of the F414 afterburner were derived from technologies developed for the F110 and YF120 engines. As this new powerplant had little parts in common with the F404 it was decided to re-designate it F414.

The engine is 155.5-in long, weighs 2,445-lb, has an inlet diameter of 30.6 inches and is rated at 14,770-lb thrust at the maximum power throttle setting without the use of afterburner. At the maximum afterburner throttle setting, the engine develops 21,890-lb. of thrust, given standard day conditions of 59 degrees F and 0% humidity at sea level.

The F414 utilises dual axial flow rotor systems; a three stage fan rotor driven by a single stage low pressure turbine and a seven stage high pressure compressor rotor driven by a single stage high pressure turbine. Variable geometry vanes are employed on both rotor systems. On the fan rotor system the inlet guide vanes can be angled 45° and stage one vanes can travel a total of 10°.

The engine control system utilises a power management system, which provides nearly constant thrust throughout the engines life, while maintaining full operational capability throughout the envelope. The engine is controlled by a FADEC (Full Authority Digital Electronic Control) unit consisting of dual channel system, which allows full thrust modulation including afterburner in each channel.

The engine itself consists of six individually replaceable modules and an accessory package. The modules, the largest convenient assembly of the engine that can be removed or installed as a unit to expedite engine assembly or disassembly, are interchangeable from engine to engine. The six engine modules are as follows: 1 Fan; 2 Compressor; 3 Combustor; 4 High Pressure Turbine; 5 Low Pressure Turbine; 6 Afterburner.

General Electric Aircraft Engines F414. GEAC

The accessory gearbox is a lightweight cast aluminium housing mounted to the engine mid-frame at the six o'clock position. Mounted to, and driven by, the accessory gearbox are the following line replaceable units: a combined Engine Main and Afterburner Fuel Pump (Engine Fuel Pump), a combined Variable Exhaust Nozzle and Start Boost Pump, a Lube and Scavenge Pump, and a permanent magnet alternator. Power extracted from the engine compressor rotor is used to operate all engine gearbox mounted accessories and one of the Aircraft Mounted Accessory Drive gearboxes.

The F414 fan module, which has an inlet diameter of 30.6 inches and weighs 486-lb., is composed of the front frame, fan stator and fan rotor. The front frame controls the flow of inlet air to the fan rotor. The fan stator houses three stages of vanes, which direct the air flow to the rotor blades, completing each stage of compression. The fan rotor is a three stage rotor driven by the low pressure turbine which compresses the airflow to help in the development of thrust, as well as providing an air source for sump seal pressurisation and cooling of the core rotor, exhaust frame and variable exhaust engine nozzle.

The compressor module, which weighs in at 560-lb., is comprised of the mid-frame, compressor stator, compressor rotor, combustion chamber case, outer bypass ducts, and power takeoff assembly. The mid-frame supports the aft end of the fan rotor, forward end of the compressor rotor and the engine accessory gearbox. It also splits off fan discharge airflow into bypass and core airflow and ports off fan discharge air for internal cooling of the core rotor and oil sump pressurisation.

The compressor rotor, which is a seven-stage rotor driven by the single stage high-pressure turbine, houses six stages of vanes, which direct the air flow to the compressor rotor blades, completing each stage of compression. The combustion chamber case bolts to the aft flange of the compressor case and discharges airflow and directs it to the combustor module.

The Combustor module, which weighs approximately 86-lb., consists of the combustion liner, high-pressure turbine nozzle segments and the high-pressure turbine inner nozzle support. The Combustor module is the component that contains combustion within the engine. The high-pressure turbine nozzle segments direct the Combustor discharge airflow to the high-pressure turbine blades.

An F/A-18F from VFA-41 lands aboard the USS *Nimitz* (CVN 68) steaming in the Pacific Ocean on 22 March 2003. USN

Like many other US tactical combat aircraft the Super Hornets GE F414 engines incorporate fully convergent divergent engine nozzles. H Harkins

The high-pressure turbine module, which weighs in at 165-lb., comprised the high pressure turbine disk, the high pressure turbine blades, the high pressure turbine rotating air seal, the high pressure turbine air duct, the high pressure turbine rear shaft, the high pressure turbine seal support, the air oil separator, the rear cooling plate, and the #4 carbon seal. The high-pressure turbine module extracts energy from the combustion airflow exiting the high-pressure turbine nozzle and uses that energy to drive the seven-stage compressor rotor.

The low-pressure turbine module, which weighs 419-lb., comprises the low pressure turbine disk, the low pressure turbine blades, the forward retaining plate, the rear retaining plate, inter turbine air seal, the low pressure turbine rear shaft, the #4 roller bearing, the #4 bearing air duct, the #4 roller oil seal, the #5 bearing, the #5 bearing oil seal, the #5 bearing labyrinth seal, the low pressure stator case, the low pressure turbine shrouds, the high pressure shroud support, the high pressure turbine shrouds, and the exhaust frame. The low-pressure turbine module extracts energy from the combustion airflow exiting the high-pressure turbine nozzle and uses that energy to drive the three-stage fan rotor. The low-pressure turbine module also directs the exhaust gases into the afterburner module.

The afterburner module, which weighs 387-lb., comprises the afterburner case, the afterburner liner, the pilot spraybars and manifold, the main spraybars and manifold, the pilot and main spraybar heat-shields, and variable exhaust nozzle flaps and seals. The afterburner module provides an area where additional thrust may be periodically developed by igniting fuel injected into the exiting exhaust gases. The module utilises a convergent/divergent variable exhaust nozzle, which enables the acceleration of both subsonic as well as supersonic airflow and ensures the proper exit opening for the gas stream.

The F414 has a maximum diameter of 35-in, and a Pressure Ratio of 30 to 1. With a maximum thrust rating of almost 97.86-kN (22,000-lb) the F414 has an impressive thrust to weight ratio of 9:1, which compares well with the F404 installed in the first generation Hornet. Thrust growth is limited to 10-15%, but up to 30% more thrust is theoretically possible.

An F414 undergoes shipboard testing. USN

The first of fourteen F414 development engines was delivered for ground testing in 1993, and by the time the first flight test engine was delivered in June 1995 the F414 development program was 70% complete, with seven F414 development engines having accumulated more than 4,300 test hours. This total included more than 1,800 hours of accelerated simulated mission testing on five engines. Two F414 engines had accumulated more than 850 hours of altitude testing, during which time the engines demonstrated operability and performance throughout the flight envelope. More than 6,000 hours of F414 testing had been completed before the first F/A-18E flight in September 1995. The development program called for the 14 engines to accumulate 10,000 test hours by 1997, completing the initial engine development.

In June 2001, General Electric was awarded a $418 million contract for 86 F414-GE-400 engines. This brought to 297 the number of engines ordered as part of the procurement plan to purchase a total of 1,096 F414-GE-400 engines, plus spares, for 548 aircraft. Of the 213 F414 engines purchased through earlier contracts, 116 were in operational service supporting 47 F/A-18E/F aircraft at NAS Lemoore and China Lake in California by June 2001.

Development of the engine continued, with the goal of producing growth developments resulting in the F414 EDE (Enhanced Durability Engine), now referred to as the F414 Enhanced, which has an 18% increase in thrust and lower life cycle costs.

The higher-powered F414 engines enable the Super Hornet to carry a larger payload of 8051 kg (17,750-lb) compared with the 7031 kg (15,500-lb) of the F/A-18C. The aircraft's larger size allows an extra 1361-kg (3,000-lb) of fuel to be carried internally while an additional 1406-kg (3,100-lb) can be carried externally. This increased fuel capacity allows the F/A-18E/F's range to be increased by 38% over that of the F/A-18C/D.

A requirement for the Super Hornet was a stipulated 4082-kg (9,000-lb) weapons/fuel bring home load which is an increase of 1587 kg (3,500-lb) over the 2495-kg (5,500-lb) of the F/A-18C. Drawing on the experience of a Canadian modification for its Hornets the F/A-18E/F could carry three 1818-litre (400-Imp-gal) external fuel tanks for a maximum load of 4436-kg (9,780-lb). This tank was not adopted for the F/A-18C/D in US service as it was too large to be carried on the centreline station while the aircraft was on the ground, but as the Super Hornet stands higher on the ground there is no such restriction.

This F/A-18 Hornet was used as the Avionics Test-bed for the Super Hornet program. The aircraft is seen here landing after a development flight. NAWC-WD

F414-GE-400
Maximum Diameter: 35 in
Pressure Ratio: 30 to 1
Thrust-to-Weight: 9 to 1 Class
Milestones: F414-GE-400
EMD commenced June 1992
First F414 engine test May 1993
First flight test engine delivered June 1995
PFQ (Flight Qualification) September 1995
First F414 flight 29 November 1995
Low Rate Production Qualification September 1996
First Production Delivery June 1998

Initially the Super Hornet retained the same cockpit canopy and Martin Baker NACES ejection-seat system as installed in the F/A-18C/D. In mid-1997, it was revealed that YF-4J Phantom II BuNo.151473 was being operated by the Point Mugu Naval Weapons Test Squadron 'Bloodhounds' on trials work for a new ejection seat for the Hornet and Super Hornet. The aircraft had previously been stored at NAS China Lake. The white painted aircraft was appropriately named 'Ghost'.

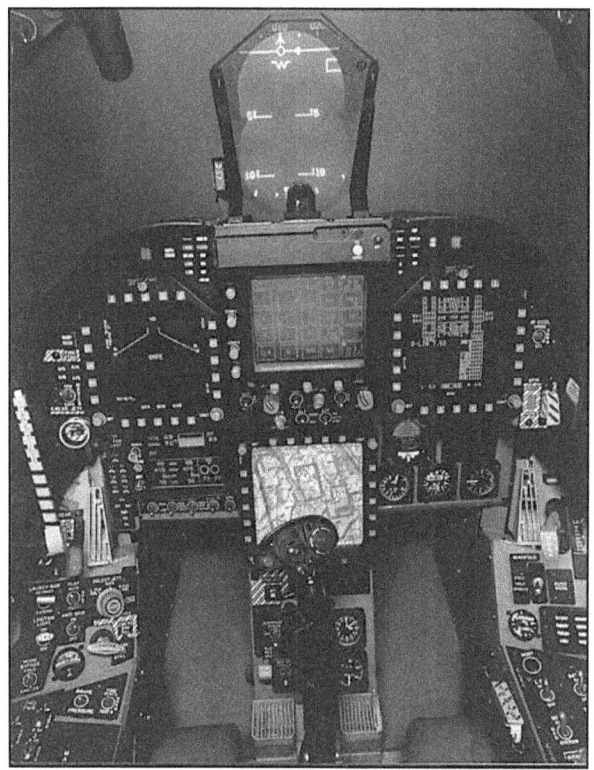

The initial Super Hornet cockpit was dominated by a single 20-cm x 20-cm square flat plate active matrix liquid crystal tactical situation display. NAWC-WD

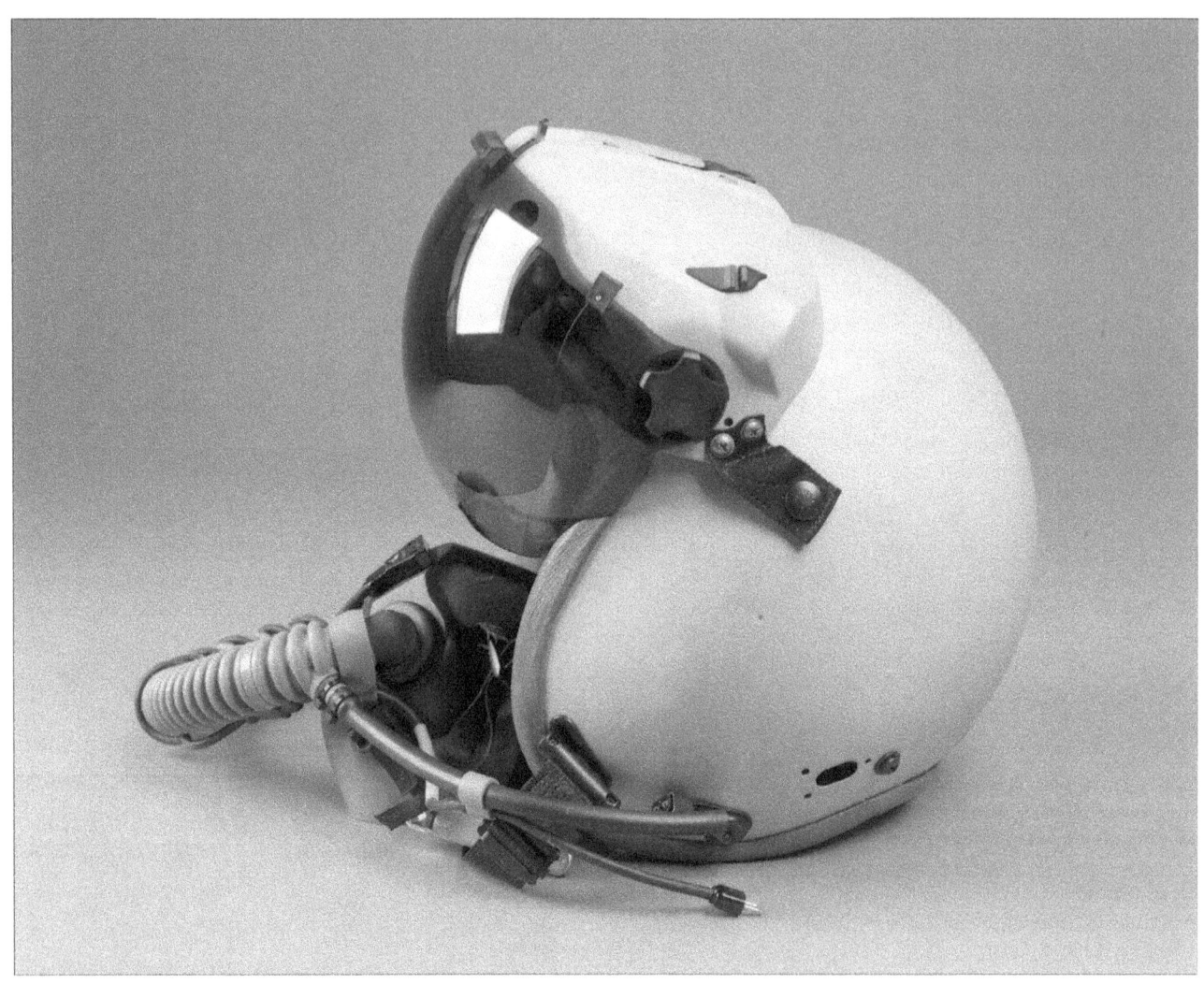

The Joint Helmet Mounted Cueing was initially aimed at cueing short-range air to air missile like the Raytheon AIM-9X Sidewinder, further enhancements allowing cueing of air surface stores such as the JDAM. Boeing

Initially the F/A-18E/F retained about 90% avionics commonality with the F/A-18C/D, with the baseline avionics suite being identical to that of the late model F/A-18C/D from Lot 19 onwards, except for the enhanced crew station.

Initially the initial cockpit of the Super Hornet retained much of the equipment found in late production F/A-18C/D's, including HOTAS (Hands on Throttle and Stick) controls. However, it also introduced new equipment. The 'C/D's' single 5-in x 5-in (12.7-cm x 12.7-cm) central display screen was replaced by a single 8-in x 8-in (20-cm x 20-cm), 200-cm-square (78.74 in-square) flat plate AMLCDS (Active-Matrix Liquid Crystal Display Screen) tactical situation display, which shows inputs from various sensors. The central LCD (Liquid Crystal Display) is produced by Kaiser, as are the two 5in x 5in screens of the 'C/D' which were retained in the Super Hornet.

In late 1999, Kaiser Electronics, a division of the Kaiser Aerospace & Electronics Corporation, was awarded a contract from Boeing for development of a projection display for the F/A-18E/F cockpit. The new display, referred to by Boeing as the Digital Expandable Colour Display (DECD), was a 6.25" x 6.25" reflective micro Liquid Crystal Display projection based smart display The DECD was developed to replace AMLCD supplied by Kaiser as part of a cost-reduction initiative for the Super Hornet program.

The Kaiser Display design was a highly rugged integration of COTS (Commercial-off-the-shelf) projector components and technologies benefiting from Kaiser Electronics experience in AMLCD head down displays and optics capabilities developed for head up and helmet mounted displays.

LRIP Super Hornets, such as this Batch 1 aircraft, were delivered with the Raytheon APG-73 radar carried over from late production F/A-18C/D. The APG-73, while being a competent radar in both air to ground and air to air scenarios, was progressively falling further behind in the ever increasing technology advancement of modern airborne radar systems. H Harkins

F/A-18F's were to be available with a missionised rear crew station from 2003, equipped with duel weapon controllers, a centrally mounted 8 x 10 in class liquid crystal display and three smaller displays. The F/A-18C/D HUD was retained in the Super Hornet, although a Kaiser touch sensitive monochrome screen replaced the push up button control panel below it.

The JHMCS (Joint Helmet Mounted Cueing System), developed by a Boeing-Vision Systems International team, was a joint USAF/USN program to field an advanced cueing system for use with all current sensors and those weapons/sensors projected to enter service in the near future. The system, which features both air-to-air and air-to-surface capability and can be employed on all US tactical combat aircraft, combines a magnetic head tracker with a display projected onto the pilot's visor, giving the pilot a targeting device that can be used to aim sensors and weapons wherever the pilot is looking. The pilot can aim the radar, air-to-air missiles, infrared sensors, and air-to-surface weapons simply by pointing his/her head at the target and pressing a switch on the flight controls. Additionally, the pilot can view any desired data (airspeed, altitude, target range, etc.) while 'heads-up', eliminating the need to look into the cockpit.

The AIM-9X is an advanced short-range dogfight weapon that can intercept airborne targets located at high off-boresight lines-of-sight relative to the 'shooter', providing a weapon with a short-range intercept envelope significantly larger than its predecessors. The HOBS (High Off-Boresight Seeker) system - the combination of JHMCS & AIM-9X seeker head - results in a weapon that can attack manoeuvring airborne targets seen by the pilot, even without manoeuvring the launch aircraft, minimising the time spent in the threat environment. The result is greater lethality, survivability and pilot situational awareness during air combat.

The F/A-18 Advanced Weapons Laboratory (the old WSSA) at China Lake, California, began developmental test flights) during October 1998. VX-9 flew some of those development sorties and then began Operational Test of the JHMCS in August 1999, in conjunction with OT-IIA (Operational Testing-IIA of the AIM-9X missile.

Boeing received USN Approval for its JHMCS to proceed to LRIP (Low-Rate Initial Production) in

July 2000, by which time around 275 test flights had been conducted to verify that the system was reliable. Flight test with the JHMCS on a Super Hornet commenced in April 2001 at the NAWC-WD and a production standard system was flown on an F/A-18F on 29 August, with 36 LRIP JHMCS systems ordered to equip Super Hornets due for delivery in fiscal year 2002.

The Super Hornet was equipped with a new digital map featuring growth for a Terrain Reference Navigation (TRN) system, which will allow the aircraft's position to be constantly updated relative to the ground by matching a library of stored terrain data with radar altimeter readings.

The navigation system comprised a Litton LN-100G integrated GPS/INS (Global-Positioning System/Inertial Navigation System), which combined a Litton LN-100 laser gyro/INS with a Rockwell-Collins GPS-receiver module; the same system selected for the F-22A Raptor and retrofitted to some F/A-18C/D's.

The APX-100 IFF (Identification Friend or Foe) installed on the early model Hornets was replaced in late model F/A-18C/D by the Hazeltine APX-113 Combined Interrogator Transponder and this system was carried over to the Super Hornet.

The Super Hornet was to be equipped with a datalink allowing information such as threats, targets, and fuel and weapon states to be shared with and received from other fighters and support aircraft. Among these would be Northrop Grumman E-2 Hawkeye, AWACS (Airborne Warning and Control System) and Boeing E-3 Sentry AWACS, as well as E-8 Joint Stars and air refuelling tankers.

The rear cockpit of the baseline F/A-18F is identical to the front except that there is no HUD and the central display screen is located above the landscape format touch screen.

The Control Data International AYK-14 core mission computer, the same system as that installed in the F/A-18C/D, drives the cockpit systems. While this has been the standard USN airborne computer since the 1980's, it has undergone significant upgrading with the XN-8 version installed in the F/A-18C/D also being installed in the seven Super Hornet prototypes. With a capacity for 2 million words of memory this system remained adequate until after the year 2000. The AYK-14 was installed in all seven-development aircraft and was fitted to the 62 LRIP aircraft in Lot 1, 2 and 3. By the time the program proceed to full rate production improved mission computers system were introduced.

The Raytheon AN/APG-73 was selected to equip production standard Super Hornets. Raytheon

As previously mentioned, initial Super Hornet retained the Raytheon (formerly Hughes) AN/APG-73 multi-role pulse Doppler radar as fitted in late model F/A-18C/D's. The APG-73 is often referred to as an improved version of the AN/APG-65 installed in the earlier Hornets, although it retains little in common with the older radar other than the antenna.

Throughout the 1980's and early 1990's Hughes continually updated the APG-65, mainly with faster processors and increased memory. By the late 1980's, however, Hughes was producing more advanced systems such as the APG-70 for the F-15E and retrofitted to some F-15C/D's. Hughes decided to embark on development of an improved radar for the F/A-18 designated APG 73. This radar incorporated much technology gained in development of radars such as the APG-70, an approach that involved little risk as most of the technology was already in existence.

The new radar was given the go-ahead in May 1990 when Hughes was awarded a $233 million-development contract in co-operation with Canada and the USN. The first production contract for 12 units being issued in June 1991, with an APG-73 first flying in an F/A-18 on 15 April 1992. The new radar was the standard unit delivered in all F/A-18C/D's from June 1994; the first two aircraft so equipped being delivered to the USN on 25 and 26 May 1994. Many earlier Hornets were equipped with the system as a retrofit, with the redundant APG-65 radars then going to equip AV-B Harrier II Plus fighters.

Like its APG-65 forebear, the APG-73 became the standard against which other radar designers had to beat throughout the 1990's. Improvements over the APG-65 include a new increased signal data processor with three times the speed and memory and wider bandwidth receiver/exciter providing faster analogue to digital conversion and allowing more advanced and capable ECCM to be used to counter jamming and enemy RWR (Radar Warning Receiver), power supply to support future growth, including provisions for an electronically scanned active-array antenna.

The APG-73 is an I/J band pulse-Doppler radar with low medium and high PRF (Pulse Repetition Frequency), long range VelS (Velocity Search), RWS (Range While Scan), TWS (Track While Scan), VS (Vertical Search), HUD, acquisition, boresight, RA (Raid Assessment), terrain following and terrain avoidance. In the air to ground role the radar has higher resolution for ground mapping and weapon delivery modes. In the raid assessment mode the APG-73 is better than the older radar at discriminating between closely spaced air to air targets. Detection range for a fighter-sized target has been increased over that of the APG-65.

The initial standard of radar, known as phase one, two additional development phases being planned for incorporation into the baseline radar. Phase two would include incorporation of a high-resolution SAR (Synthetic Aperture Radar) mode similar to that available on APG-70, which uses a technique, which emulates the resolution of a very large antenna by using the aircraft's movements between pulses. Problems with the accuracy of the SAR mode on the APG-73 were overcome by incorporating a Honeywell ring-laser gyro IMU (Inertial Measurement Unit). The SAR mode was first fitted the ATARS equipped F/A-18D's for the USMC.

Phase 3 radar development would introduce an active-array antenna replacing the traditional nodding antenna fitted on current sets. The active-array comprises hundreds of transmit/receive modules. As well as the advantages of faster mode changes and beam steering the active-array can also be stealthier than the mechanical systems as the active-array can be shaped to reduce the radar signature. The AESA program eventually matured into the APG-79.

> **AN/APG-65/73** - The AN/APG-65 is highly reliable, flexible all-weather multi-mode sensor that is used for both air-to-air and air-to-surface missions. The key to the APG-65's flexibility is its programmable digital computers. The built-in test system provides total end-to-end radar pre-flight checkout and continuous monitoring. During air-to-air operations, the radar incorporates clean scope, look-down/shoot-down capabilities. It features complete search track and automatic acquisition modes such as high pulse repetition frequency (PRF) velocity search, high/medium PRF range-while-search, single target track, and a track-while-scan mode that tracks 10 targets simultaneously and displays eight targets. For air-to-surface operations, the radar provides Doppler beam sharpened sector and patch mapping, medium range synthetic aperture radar, "real-beam" ground mapping modes, fixed and moving ground target track, air-to-surface ranging, terrain avoidance, precision velocity update, and a sea surface search mode with clutter suppression. The re-programmable AN/APG-73 radar responds to new threats and accommodates future modes and weapons through software changes rather than hardware retrofit. The APG-73 is an all-weather, coherent, multi-mode, multi-waveform search-and-track sensor that uses programmable digital processors to provide the features and flexibility needed for both air-to-air and air-to-surface missions. An upgrade of the APG-65 that provides higher -throughputs, greater memory capacity, improved reliability, and easier maintenance without associated increases in size or weight.
>
> Phase II of the upgrade completed development. It incorporates a motion sensing subsystem with reconnaissance software, a stretch waveform generator module, and a special test equipment instrumentation and reconnaissance module. These enhancements give the F/A-18 capability to make high-resolution radar ground maps comparable with F-15E and the U-2, and be able to perform precision strike missions using advanced image correlation algorithms.
> Raytheon

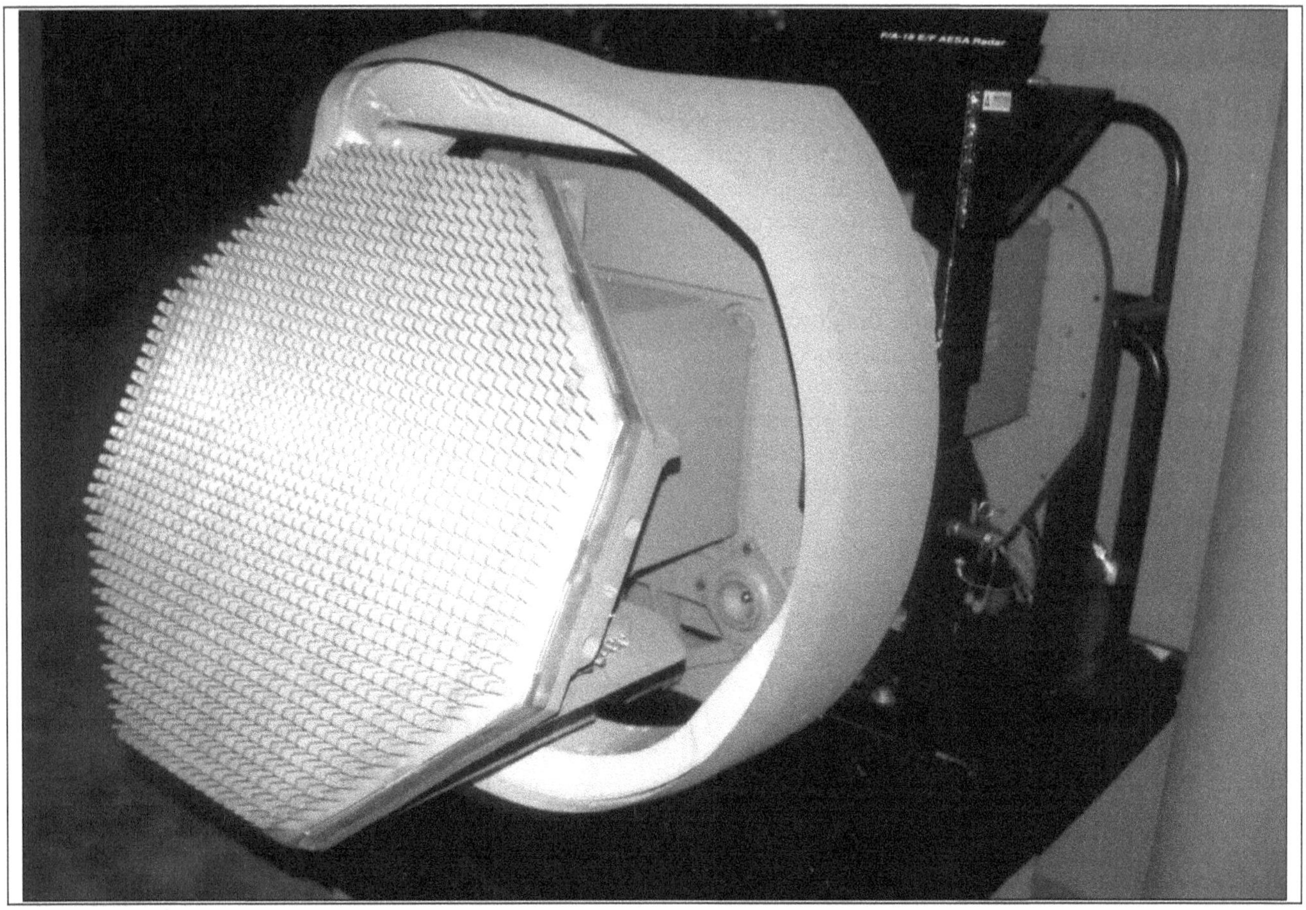

Above and right: Raytheon displayed a full-scale model of its AN/APG-79 Advanced Electronically Scanned Array radar at Farnborough in July 2000. H Harkins

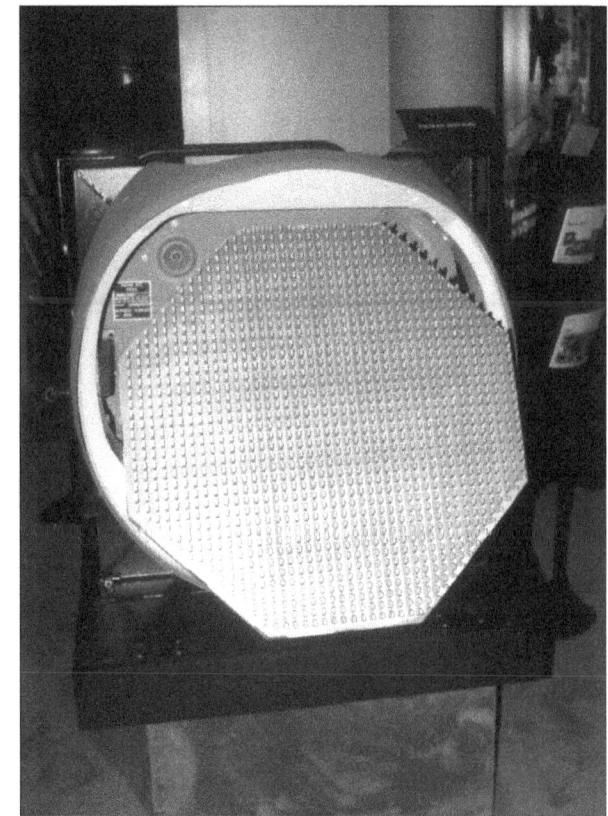

In 1998, the USN was looking at the possible acquisition of a new AESA (Active Electronically Scanned Array) radar for its planned F/A-18E/F fleet. In March 1999, Northrop Grumman began flight testing what it described as a 'fourth generation' AESA radar and was preparing its bid for the USN requirement for the Super Hornet. The new AESA radar, which was flight tested in Northrop Grumman's BAC One Eleven flying test-bed, was claimed to be well in advance of the Raytheon AN/APG-77 being developed for the Lockheed Martin F-22, which Northrop Grumman described as 'third generation'. Northrop Grumman began work on the AESA in 1997 and in 1999 stated that a further 5 to 6 years of development was still required before the radar would be ready for production. This schedule fitted in well with the USN Super Hornet radar requirement, which had still to receive funding at that time.

Close up of the forward undercarriage gear of an F/A-18F.
Hugh Harkins

Raytheon's Electronic Systems unit in El Segundo, California, was competing with Northrop Grumman in developing AESA radar technology and in November 1999, Boeing selected Raytheon to develop the AESA radar for the Super Hornet. The announcement followed the completion of a competitive evaluation that had commenced in September 1999.

Incorporation of the AESA radar was intended to improve the survivability, capability and lethality of the Super Hornet. Specifically, the AESA increases the aircraft's air-to-air target detection and tracking range, and adds higher resolution air-to-ground mapping modes at longer ranges, enabling the aircraft to take full advantage of current and planned weapons; improves situational awareness in the cockpit and significantly lowers operating and support costs. Under an advance agreement between Boeing and the USN, Boeing and its subcontractor Raytheon would develop an integrated AESA radar prototype. Funding for the AESA program was included in the FY 2000 budget.

In February 2001 Milestone II authorisation for the AESA, which received the designation AN/APG-79, was granted for the program to enter the engineering manufacture and development phase. Following the Milestone II decision a $324 (approximately) million contract was awarded to Boeing for the design, development, fabrication, integration, installation and test of five full and two partial AESA radar engineering development models.

The AESA active electronic beam scanning allows very fast radar beam steering and the agile beam enables the radar "to interleave in near-real time, so that the pilot and crew can use both modes simultaneously". "... the APG-79 demonstrates reliability, image resolution, and targeting and tracking range significantly greater than that of the previous mechanically scanned array F/A-18 radar. With its open systems architecture and compact, commercial-off-the-shelf part, it delivers dramatically increased capability in a smaller, lighter package. The array is composed of numerous solid-state transmit and receive modules to virtually eliminate mechanical breakdown. Other systems components include an advanced receiver/exciter, ruggedized COTS processor, and power supplies." - Raytheon

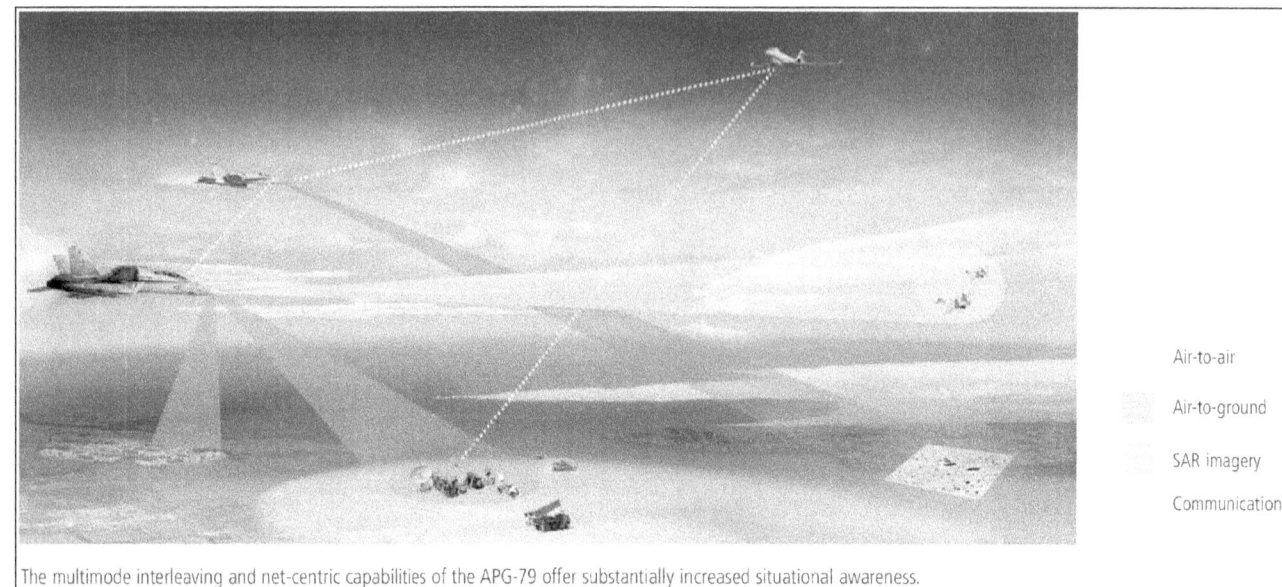

The multimode interleaving and net-centric capabilities of the APG-79 offer substantially increased situational awareness.

- Air-to-air
- Air-to-ground
- SAR imagery
- Communication

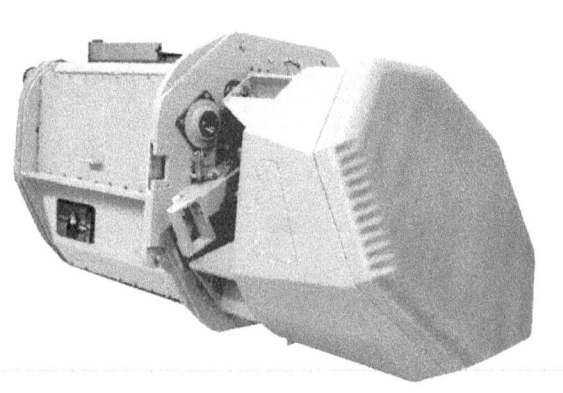

Capabilities

- Agile beam forming (permits thousands of beam positions per second)
- Interleaved radar modes, including air-to-air and air-to-ground
- Multiple radar modes, including:
  - Real beam mapping
  - Synthetic aperture radar
  - Air-to-air search
  - Air-to-air track
  - Sea surface search
  - Ground moving target indication/track

Design Features

- Solid-state digital radar with agile moving beam
- Lightweight, highly reliable tile array architecture
- Modular software and hardware, including weapon replaceable assemblies
- Ruggedized COTS-based common integrated sensor processor
- Multi-channel receiver/exciter with programmable waveforms
- Designed to support FORCEnet, the U.S. Navy's vision for a fully networked battlespace

Specifications

Platform	F/A-18E/F Super Hornet (approved for international customers)
Reliability	>15,000 hr MTBCF array, >1,250 hr MTBCF system
Weight	95 lb array, 650 lb total system weight

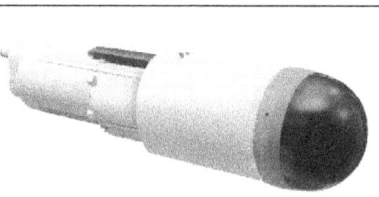

Specifications

Field of Regard
- Azimuth ±70 deg
- Elevation ±70 deg

Infrared Reciever
- Diameter 9.2 in
- Length 38 in
- Weight 115 lb

Processor
- Height 9.0 in / 8.2 in
- Length 19.0 in / 8.5 in
- Width 10.4 in / 12.1 in
- Weight 69 lb / 33 lb

Left: Graphic outlining the basic features of the APG-79 AESA. Raytheon

Above: Graphic outlining the basic features of the IRST installed in the Super Hornet. Lockheed Martin

F/A-18F1 takes the wire as it comes aboard the aircraft carrier USS *John C Stennis*. USN

Until its retirement in September 2006, the USN had an IRST (Infrared Search and Track) capability on its F-14D Tomcat fighters, operating 62 AN/AAS-42 systems. This capability was lost when the Tomcat was retired, with no plans to introduce a similar system on the F/A-18F proper, but provision has been made for installation of a Lockheed Martin IRST21 in the nose of the centreline fuel tank. This system, flight tested in 2014 and scheduled for deployment in 2017, features "long-range infrared scan and detection of airborne threats, passive detection and ranging, large field of regard, immune to electronic deception, programmable scan modes, low false alarm rate, and automatic target detection algorithms".

Many Russian and European 4th Plus and 5th Generation fighters in service or development employ advanced IRST systems enabling the detection, track and engagement of a target without the target being aware of the threat. The USAF currently does not operate, nor does it have plans to fit such a system to its existing legacy fighters (prior to F-35), possibly shying away from such systems are they are a highly effective way of countering 'stealth' aircraft and the USAF does not want to beat the drum for a system that can counter a technology on which it has invested so much.

The IDECM (Integrated Defensive Electronic Counter measures) system integrates the radar with the various jamming, decoy and warning systems. This IDECM consists of a Raytheon ALR-67(V)3 RWR, a Raytheon ALE-50 towed decoy and Tracor ALE-47 'smart' chaff/flare dispenser. Some of these systems entered service on late production F/A-18C/D's prior to incorporation on the F/A-18E/F.

The ALR-67(V)3, which was delivered for use on F/A-18C/D's from FY1997, replaced the ALR-67(V)2 RWR, and with its advanced receiver and more powerful processor is much more capable of detecting dense clusters of targets which can frequency-hop. The system is also much more capable of detecting and tracking the latest generation of pulse-Doppler and monopulse radar.

The Tracor ALE-47 countermeasure dispenser, which replaced the ALE-39 in earlier generation Hornets, was introduced from 1995 (on F/A-18C/D's delivered to Finland) and on F/A-18C/D's delivered to the USN from 1996. The system comprises four 30 tube dispensers.

The Super Hornet undercarriage was strengthened to take the higher operating weights compared with the F/A-18C/D. USN

The other major component of the IDECM system is the Raytheon AN/ALE-50 TRD (Towed Radar Decoy) system, which is stowed between the jet pipes, containing 3 decoys, each of which is towed on a 100-m (328-ft) long cable. Once deployed the decoy can counter monopulse tracking-radar by emitting a signal return that mimics that of the target aircraft.

In short the AN/LE-50 is designed to act as a more appealing target than the mother aircraft, effectively luring the homing missile away from the mother aircraft, making it a highly important end-game electronic countermeasure. Although the system has been used operationally in a number of campaigns, it has never been deployed against a modern air defence system. Later versions of the ALE-50 have a new improved decoy system towed on a fibre-optic cable developed by Lockheed Martin Sanders.

The IDECM RFCM (Radio-Frequency Counter Measures) system consists of the expendable fibre-optic towed decoy linked by fibre-optic cable to an on-board technique generator. The system is intended to defeat active-radar guided air to air missiles targeted against the mother aircraft. As well as the F/A-18E/F the system is integrated on other strategic and tactical platforms including the Boeing (formerly Rockwell) B-1B Lancer, which was the first aircraft to employ the system operationally when B-1B's deployed to RAF Fairford in the UK for Operation Allied Force, the air campaign against Serbia from March to June 1999 flew bombing missions during which the ALE-50 was deployed successfully.

The IDECM allows the aircrew to respond against threats. According to Lockheed Martin Sanders the IDECM RFCM is more than a good 'missile magnet'. It breaks the paradigm by removing the distinction between traditional on-board co-herd jammers and game only repeaters. The best characteristics of both are integrated in one affordable advanced system. IDECM goes further to fill survivability gaps created by home on jam ECCM, and man in the loop command guided threats to provide robust self-protection capability. IDECM priorities are to protect the aircraft and preserve mission integrity, in doing so IDECM provides three layers of defence, 1. Suppression to deny, delay and degrade adversary acquisition and tracking, 2. Deception to mislead guided weapons away from the aircraft if a track solution is obtained and a launch occurs, 3. No game capabilities that make the fibre-optic towed decoy the preferred target, seducing adversary missiles that manage to leak through the first and second layers of defence.

In March 2001, Boeing received a $69 million contract from the USN for low rate production of 15 ATFLIR systems and spares, covering 14 pods for the F/A-18E/F and 1 pod for the F/A-18C/D. A further LRIP contract was awarded in 2002.

ATFLIR provides a significant increase in resolution and a greater magnification over previous systems like the NightHawk; these systems being 4 x and 30 x respectively. The ATFLIR system, which incorporates a visible light camera (electro-optical sensor), is a 'third generation' systems which provides the crew with the capability to detect, classify and track air to air and air to ground targets. An additional requirement was to provide autonomous precision targeting co-ordinates to 'smart' weapons such as the JSOW (Joint stand-off Weapon), JDAM (Joint Direct Attack Munitions and JASSM (Joint Air to Surface Stand-off Missile).

An F/A-18E catapults from the aircraft carrier USS *Abraham Lincoln* in February 2003. USN

IDECM takes advantage of technology developed for previous government funded programs including the ITT/Westinghouse ALQ-165 Airborne self-protection Jammer and ALE-150 developments. The system has built-in test equipment, two-level maintenance, and has been designed so that a single person can remove all modules. The system receiver weighs 14.7-kg (32.5-lb.), modulator 13.3-kg (29.3-lb.), processor, 16.5-kg (36.5-lb.), rack 21.3-kg (47.0-lb.) and SCA 5.8-kg (12.9-lb.).

The Super Hornet can be equipped with a navigation and targeting FLIR (Forward Looking Infra-Red) pod to enhance its combat effectiveness. For its planned Super Hornet fleet the USN wanted a new navigation and targeting pod to replace the AAS-38B NightHawk used by the F/A-18C/D, and on 10 November 1997, Boeing selected Hughes (now Raytheon) to develop the ASQ-228 ATFLIR (Advanced Targeting Forward-Looking InfraRed) sensor for the F/A-18 Hornet and Super Hornet, the first flight of the system on an F/A-18 taking place at the NAWC-WD, China Lake, in late November 1999.

Top: A development ATFLIR pod is nestled under the port shoulder station of a NWTS F/A-18 Hornet at China Lake. Above: The first flight of an F/A-18 with an ATFLIR pod was conducted over the China Lake ranges in November 1999. NAWC-WD

The ATFLIR is carried on the port shoulder station as seen on this F/A-18F. H Harkins

For the reconnaissance role the Super Hornet can be equipped with a pod mounted system called SHARP (Shared Reconnaissance Pod) similar to the ATARS system employed by some late model F/A-18C/D's. The Super Hornet/SHARP combination has effectively replaced the F-14/TARPS (Tactical Air Reconnaissance Pod System) in Carrier Air Wings, providing a capable day night high and medium altitude tactical reconnaissance system out to ranges of about 45 nautical miles, providing high-resolution imagery for real/near-real time reconnaissance. It is equipped with a long-range EO/IR (Electro-Optical/InfraRed) sensor; or a medium range EO/IR sensor and a real time data link that is compatible with the DGGS (Distributed Common Ground Station). The design incorporates a rotating mid-section to optimise coverage, to protect the window by allowing stowage under the strongback, and to reduce the size and life cycle expense of large fixed windows.

The pod, which weighs approximately 2,100-lb., is 188-in in length, with a height and width of 29-in, is carried on the F/A-18E/F centreline station.

The first of three prototype SHARP pods was flown on 24 March 2001 on F/A-18E2, with the pod installed on the centreline station. The testing, completed on 10 April 2001, consisted of 96 test points conducted over nine flights for a total of 13.2 flight hours. The SHARP system was deployed in 2003 on the F/A-18F's of VFA-41 aboard the USS *Nimitz*.

The second prototype tow-seat aircraft, F/A-18F2, flying over the St Louis Arch. Boeing

AE1 (AW) DARYL STORLE
"SOY"

CAPT ZACK MAY
"SHEETS"

Previous page top: A SHARP pod is prepared on an F/A-18F of VFA-41 aboard the aircraft carrier USS *Nimitz* (CVN 68). USN **Previous page bottom: F/A-18F cockpit canopy in the open position.** Author

Above: F/A-18F2, equipped with a SHARP pod on the centreline station, flies over the Pentagon in August 2001. It was once assumed that ATARS would be carried over to the F/A-18E/F; however, the internal ATARS would have required a costly redesign of the forward fuselage. This resulted in the SHARP system being developed for the larger Super Hornet. NAWC-WD

An ATARS image of San Francisco Bay. The SHARP system promised to be equally capable in the reconnaissance role. USN F-18AWL

The Super Hornet, while not being a 'stealth' aircraft in the class of the Lockheed F-117A Nighthawk or the F-22A Raptor, does incorporate measures to reduce its radar signature. Stealth technology developed for the Northrop B-2A Spirit bomber, General Dynamics/McDonnell Douglas A-12 Avenger II and Northrop/McDonnell Douglas YF-23 Advanced Tactical Fighter contender has been incorporated, notably on the wing leading edge, to augment the beneficial effect of skinning with large areas of non radar reflecting carbon epoxy. The aircraft's radar cross section has been quoted as equivalent to 1.19 m sq. (12.8 sq. ft.), which is roughly the same as the smaller F-16C/D Fighting Falcon.

The most obvious design change to improve the stealth qualities is the change to larger rectangular inlets for the F414 engines. The inlets are angled downwards and outwards to direct the radar return 'spikes' away from the nose-on aspect. Less obvious is the use of fixed, airframe mounted, radial vanes forward of the engine to prevent radar energy reaching the rotating fan. Other features designed to reduce radar signature include serrated edges on the main undercarriage and engine-access doors and diamond shaped, laser-drilled, metal screens covering all apertures and coatings and other surface treatments.

Even before the official roll out of the prototype, the manufactures were turning their attention to other potential variants of the F/A-18E/F. On 7 August 1995, McDonnell Douglas announced that an EW (Electronic Warfare) variant of the F-18F two-seat variant of the Super Hornet was being developed by McDonnell Douglas and Northrop Grumman on a private venture basis using company funding to conduct tests including wind tunnel testing. Both companies (Boeing having taken over MDC in 1997) were pushing hard for USN funding to begin development of what was termed the Command and Control Warfare (C2W) variant in 1999. Both parties signed an agreement to jointly develop the F-18F (then unofficially known as the F-18G 'Growler' or EF-18G/E/A-18G) C2W aircraft to eventually replace the Northrop Grumman E/A-6B Prowler in USN service. Details of the EA-18G variant are given in Chapter 8.

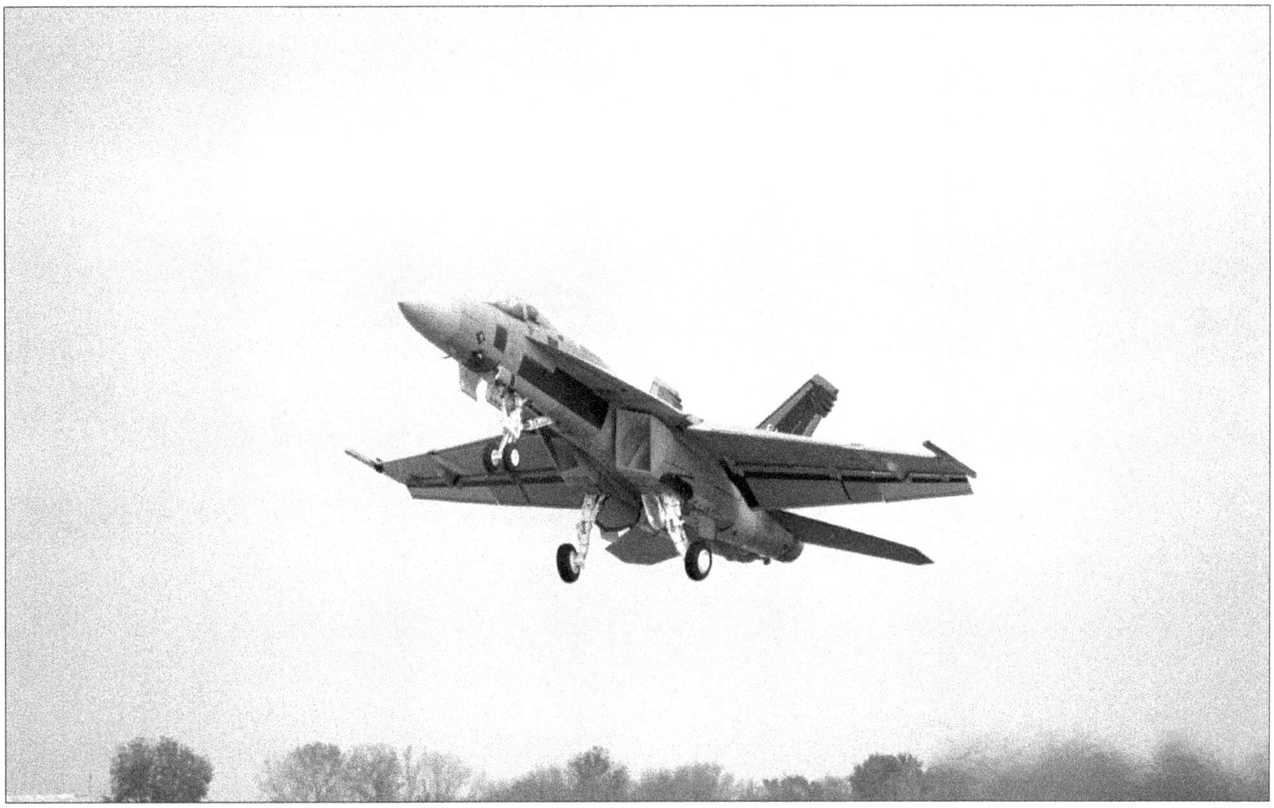

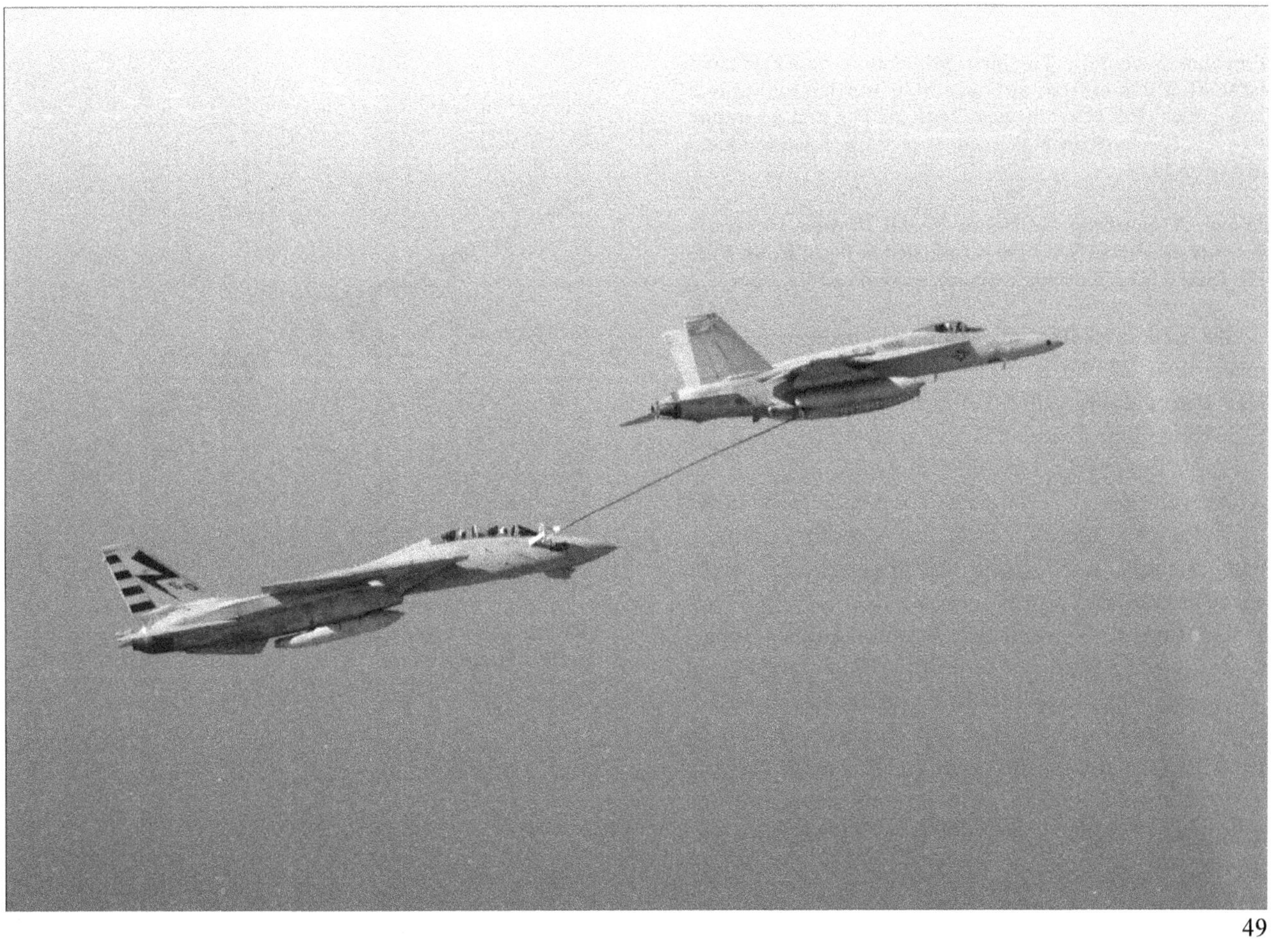

Previous page top: The first production Super Hornet, F/A-18E6, lifts of from St Louis on its maiden flight on 26 November 1998. Previous page bottom: The first prototype, F/A-18E1, refuels an F-14 Tomcat over the Atlantic Ocean in March 1999. Boeing

Above: A Northrop Grumman EA-6B Prowler Electronic Warfare aircraft of VAQ 139 is refuelled in flight by an F/A-18F from VFA 154 during a demonstration in 2011. USN

The tanker configured Super Hornet can carry more than 29,000 pounds of fuel, including up to four external 480-gallon tanks and a 330-gallon ARS (Air Refuelling Store). Fuel is transferred from the aircraft's internal and external fuel tanks through the ARS to the receiving aircraft. The Super Hornet can to fly at the same speed as the aircraft it refuels, protect itself from enemy fire, transfer fuel to the strike aircraft and return unescorted.

The first aerial refuelling from a Super Hornet tanker was performed from F/A-18E2 carrying an ARS and using F/A-18B and C models as receiver aircraft. The Super Hornet successfully refuelled an F-14 Tomcat for the first time on 11 March 1999, at an altitude of 25,000 ft., other aircraft being refuelled at altitudes ranging from 2,000 ft. to 35,000 ft.

The first prototype Super Hornet, F/A-18E1, during EMD flight testing. DoD

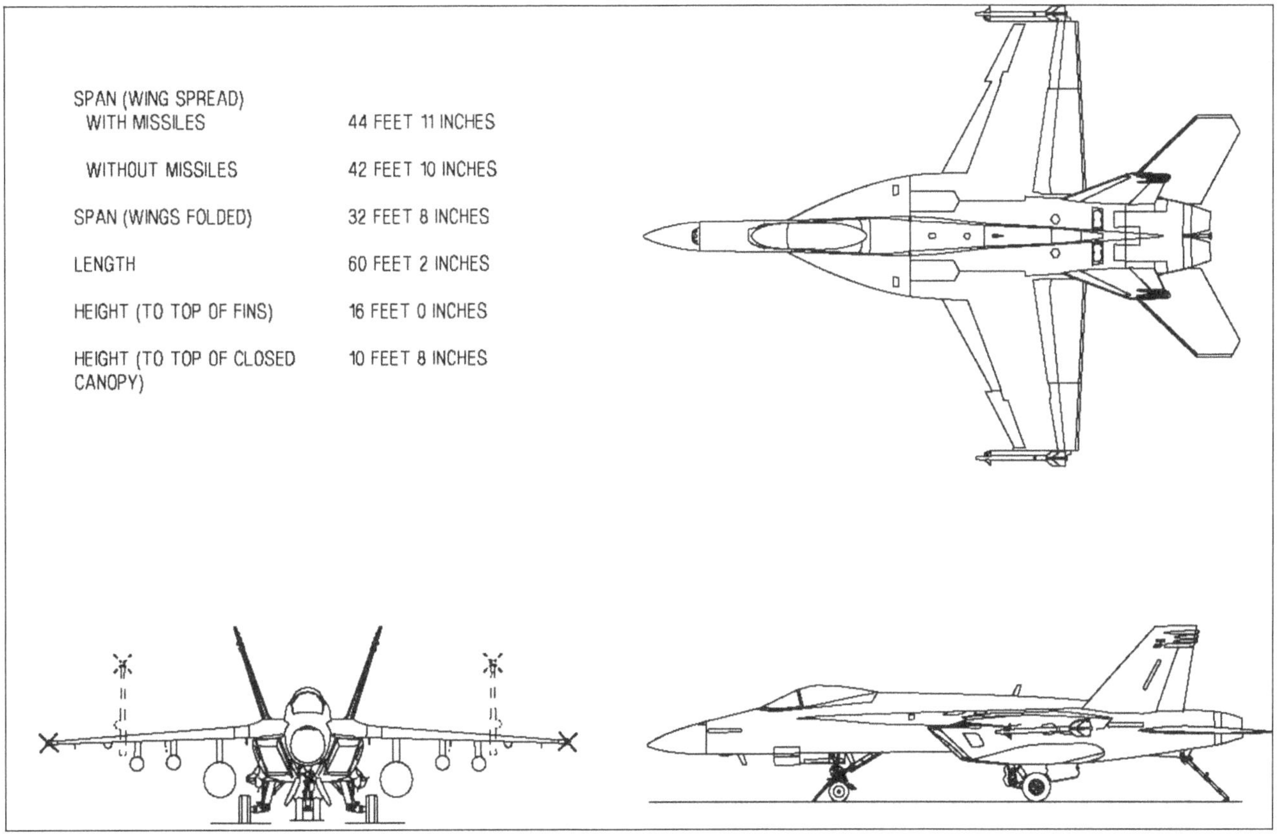

SPAN (WING SPREAD)
WITH MISSILES 44 FEET 11 INCHES
WITHOUT MISSILES 42 FEET 10 INCHES
SPAN (WINGS FOLDED) 32 FEET 8 INCHES
LENGTH 60 FEET 2 INCHES
HEIGHT (TO TOP OF FINS) 16 FEET 0 INCHES
HEIGHT (TO TOP OF CLOSED CANOPY) 10 FEET 8 INCHES

TANK 1
F/A-18F
VERTICAL FIN VENT TANK
FUSELAGE VENT TANK
ENGINES
TANK 3 (RIGHT ENGINE FEED)
TANK 4
WING FUEL TANK
TANK 2 (LEFT ENGINE FEED)
TANK 1
AIR REFUELING PROBE
DFIRS
LIQUID COOLING UNIT
WING FUEL TANK
BOARDING LADDER
OBOGS CONCENTRATOR
GUN
RADAR
SECONDARY POWER SYSTEM
● APU
● LEFT AND RIGHT AMAD

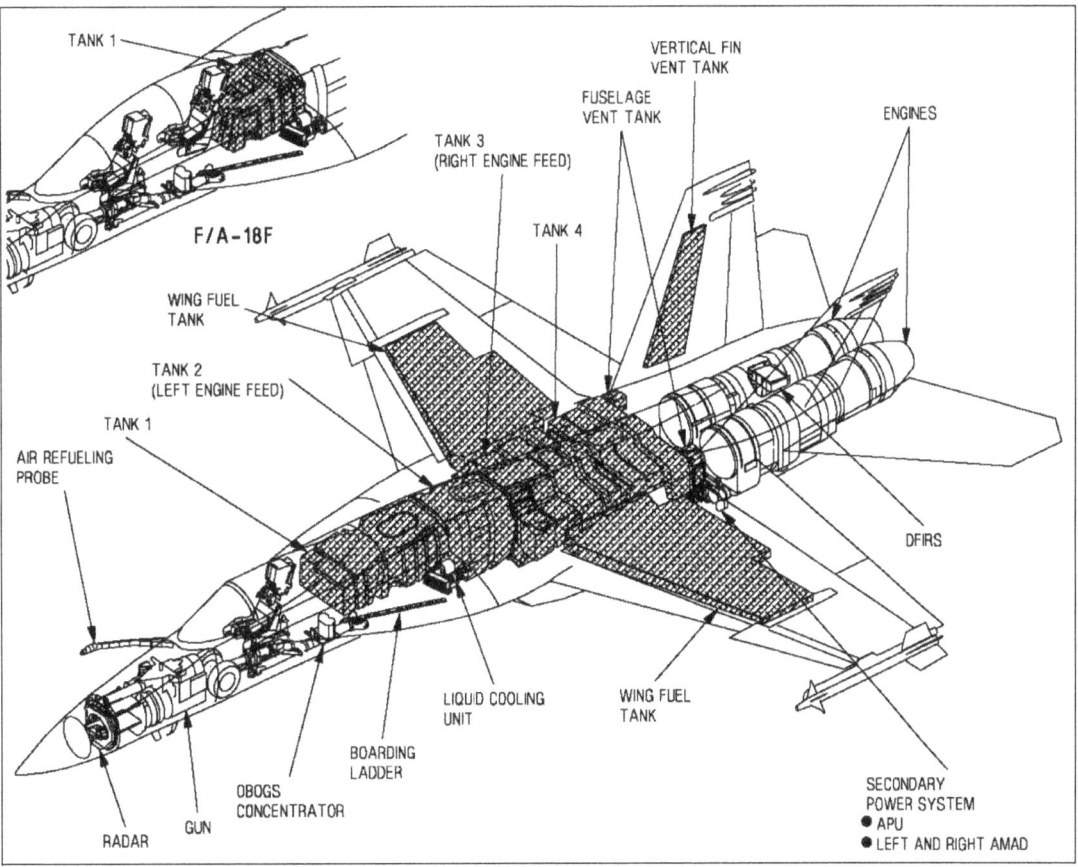

Above: General arrangement three-view of the Block 1 F/A-18E Super Hornet. NAVAIR

Left: Cutaway showing the main areas and systems of the Block 1 Super Hornet. NAVAIR

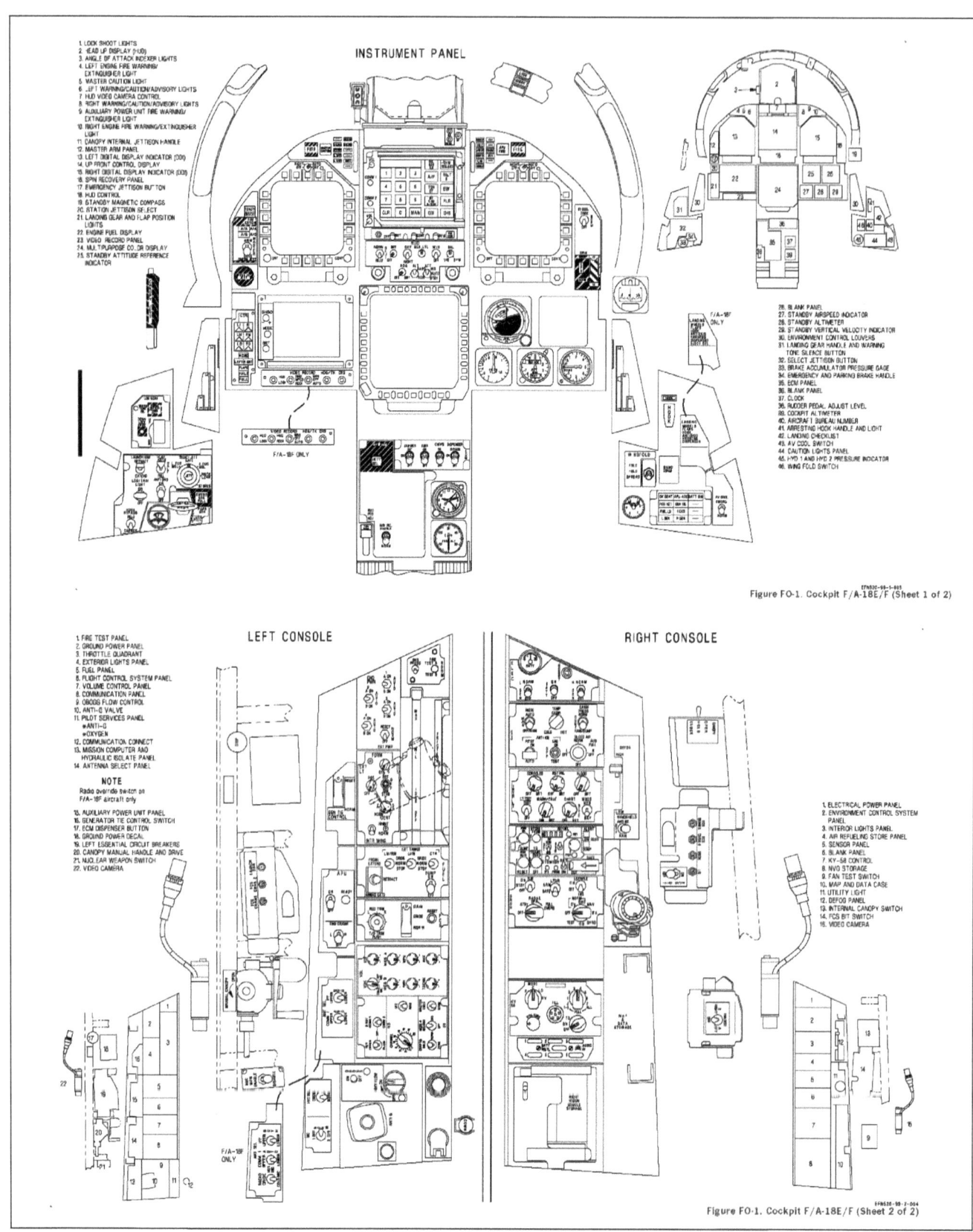

The cockpit of the Block 1 F/A-18E/F Super Hornet. NAVAIR

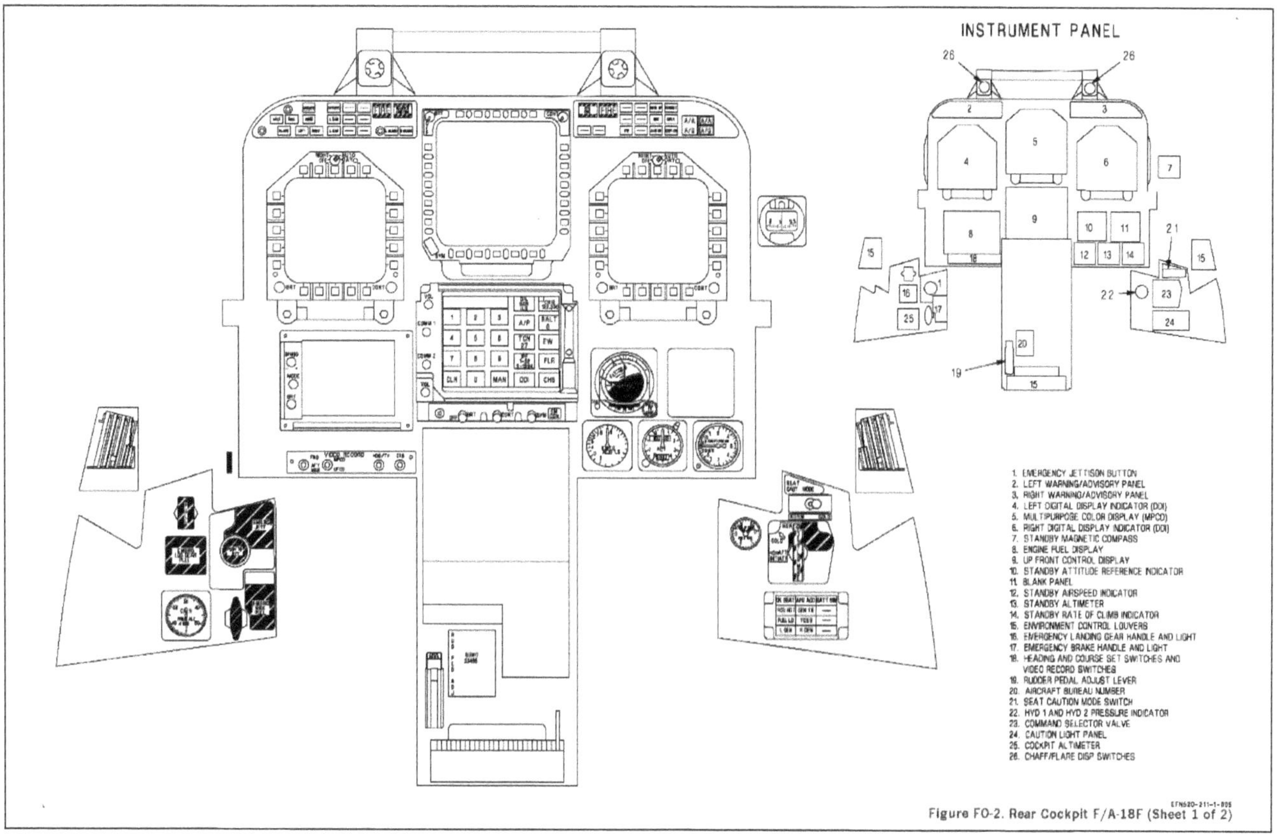
INSTRUMENT PANEL
1. EMERGENCY JETTISON BUTTON
2. LEFT WARNING/ADVISORY PANEL
3. RIGHT WARNING/ADVISORY PANEL
4. LEFT DIGITAL DISPLAY INDICATOR (DDI)
5. MULTIPURPOSE COLOR DISPLAY (MPCD)
6. RIGHT DIGITAL DISPLAY INDICATOR (DDI)
7. STANDBY MAGNETIC COMPASS
8. ENGINE FUEL DISPLAY
9. UP FRONT CONTROL DISPLAY
10. STANDBY ATTITUDE REFERENCE INDICATOR
11. BLANK PANEL
12. STANDBY AIRSPEED INDICATOR
13. STANDBY ALTIMETER
14. STANDBY RATE OF CLIMB INDICATOR
15. ENVIRONMENT CONTROL LOUVERS
16. EMERGENCY LANDING GEAR HANDLE AND LIGHT
17. EMERGENCY BRAKE HANDLE AND LIGHT
18. HEADING AND COURSE SET SWITCHES AND VIDEO RECORD SWITCHES
19. RUDDER PEDAL ADJUST LEVER
20. AIRCRAFT BUREAU NUMBER
21. SEAT CAUTION MODE SWITCH
22. HYD 1 AND HYD 2 PRESSURE INDICATOR
23. COMMAND SELECTOR VALVE
24. CAUTION LIGHT PANEL
25. COCKPIT ALTIMETER
26. CHAFF/FLARE DISP SWITCHES
EFN620-211-1-005
Figure FO-2. Rear Cockpit F/A-18F (Sheet 1 of 2)

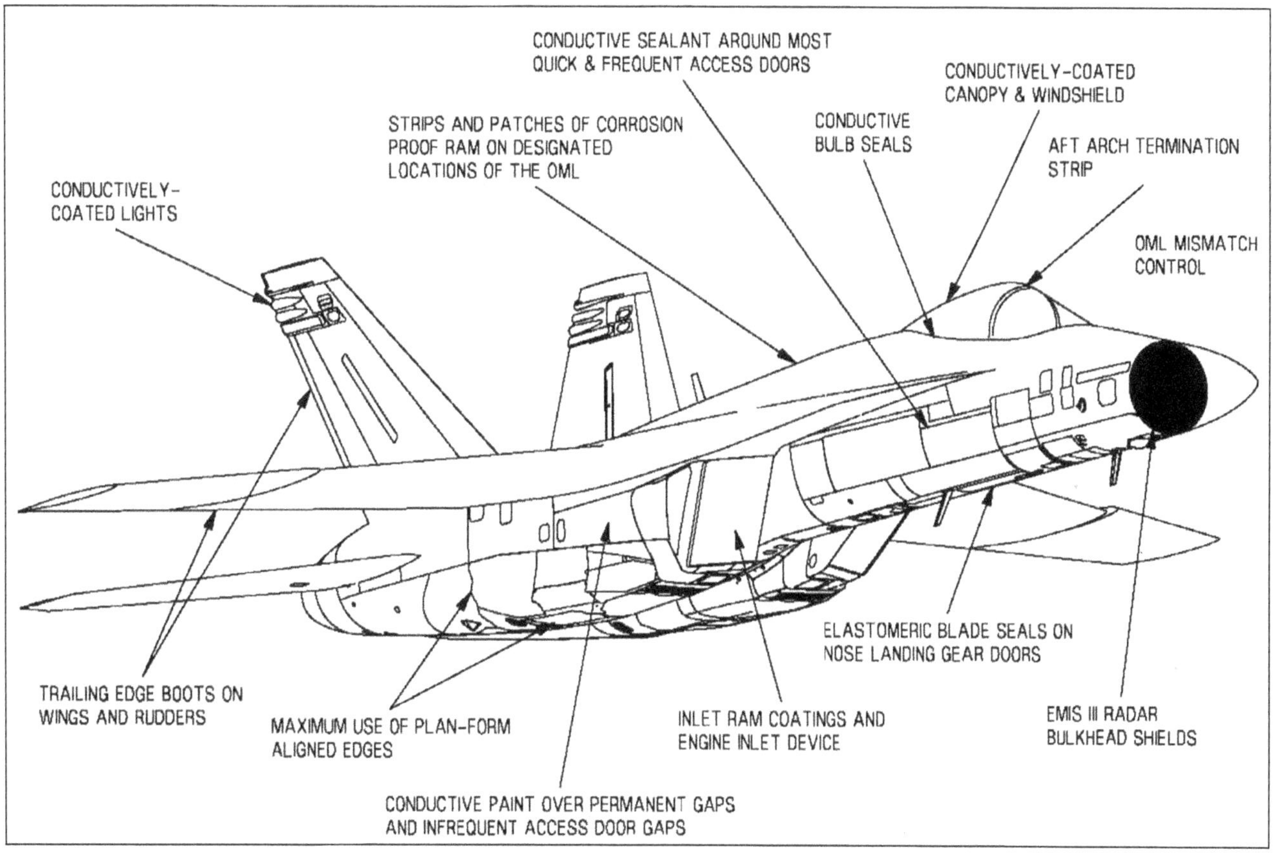
CONDUCTIVE SEALANT AROUND MOST QUICK & FREQUENT ACCESS DOORS
CONDUCTIVELY-COATED CANOPY & WINDSHIELD
STRIPS AND PATCHES OF CORROSION PROOF RAM ON DESIGNATED LOCATIONS OF THE OML
CONDUCTIVE BULB SEALS
AFT ARCH TERMINATION STRIP
CONDUCTIVELY-COATED LIGHTS
OML MISMATCH CONTROL
ELASTOMERIC BLADE SEALS ON NOSE LANDING GEAR DOORS
TRAILING EDGE BOOTS ON WINGS AND RUDDERS
MAXIMUM USE OF PLAN-FORM ALIGNED EDGES
INLET RAM COATINGS AND ENGINE INLET DEVICE
EMIS III RADAR BULKHEAD SHIELDS
CONDUCTIVE PAINT OVER PERMANENT GAPS AND INFREQUENT ACCESS DOOR GAPS

Top: Rear cockpit of the F/A-18F Block 1. Above: F/A-18E Block 1 Radar Cross Section Reduction measures. NAVAIR

Raytheon's solution for air combat in the first decade of the 21st Century. The AIM-120C AMRAAM at top of picture and the AIM-9X Sidewinder bottom. Hugh Harkins

The Super Hornet was intended to operate with many existing weapons along with the new generation of air to air and air to surface weapons then being developed. The primary air to air missile would be the AIM-120 AMRAAM which was designed as a direct replacement for the AIM-7 Sparrow semi-active radar homing missile. Smaller, lighter and faster than its predecessor, AMRAAM revolutionised NATO air-to-air capability, being able to operate in three modes depending on target range and conditions of engagement. Once launched the missile flies towards the target under control of the pre-programmed inertial guidance system, requiring no further assistance from the launch aircraft. For long-range engagements the aircraft can update the missile flight path mid-course, transmitting target location data to the missile guidance section, following which it goes into autonomous mode, using inertial guidance only. Once near the target it switches to terminal homing mode using the on board active monopulse radar seeker. Unlike the vintage Sparrow, which required the launch aircraft to continually keep the target illuminated by its radar during the missile flight time, AMRAAM has its own on-board active-homing radar, together with an INS and a data-link and the missile can be used to engage multiple targets simultaneously whereas with Sparrow only one target could be engaged at a time.

AMRAAM has a similar configuration to Sparrow with four fixed central wings and four rear control fins. The missile is smaller and lighter than its predecessor with a length of 3.65 m, a diameter of 17.8 cm, wing span 44.5 cm, fin span 44.7 cm and weighs in at 161.5 kg, including the 20.5 kg warhead, with either a proximity or contact fuse (note: figures are for the AIM-120C-5). Powered by a solid propellant rocket motor the missile has a speed of Mach 3 and a maximum range of 65-km (40.4 miles), being faster and having a longer engagement range than its predecessor, and also more manoeuvrable and more resistant to ECM. As long as the launch aircraft has a track while scan radar up to six missiles can be fired in rapid succession against separate targets.

AMRAAM entered service with the USAF in 1991 and with the USN on F/A-18 Hornets a few years later This Super Hornet is carrying 4 AMRAAM's and a pair of AIM-9M's. Boeing

AMRAAM was designed in the 1970's and the conceptual phase of the program was completed in February 1979 when two of five competing contractors (Hughes and Raytheon) were selected by the USAF to continue to the 33-month validation phase, during which both contractors produced hardware to support their respective concepts. In December 1981, the validation phase of the program was concluded when both contractors apparently demonstrated that their respective flight-test missiles could meet the USAF/USN requirements. The USAF, as the full-scale developer, selected Hughes Missile Systems group and Raytheon was selected as a follower producer and in 1987, Hughes and Raytheon received production contracts for AMRAAM missiles.

AMRAAM entered service in time to be employed operationally during the 1991 Gulf War; however no missiles were launched before the cease-fire. AMRAAM has been used in several engagements by US and NATO forces against Iraqi and Serbian aircraft since 1992, with mixed results. The first combat use occurred on 27 December 1992 when a USAF F-16D Block 42 fighter launched an AMRAAM from BVR at an Iraqi MiG-25 'Foxbat' E in the controversial no fly zone over Southern Iraq, the missile destroying the Iraqi aircraft.

The Pre-Planned Product Improvement (P3I) program was designed to ensure capability was sustained throughout the missiles service life. The first two phases included clipped wings and fins for the AIM-120C to allow it to be carried internally in the F-22 Raptor, an improved warhead and fuse, enhanced ECCM (Electronic Counter Counter Measures) capability and a reduced length, SCAS (Shortened Control and Actuation Section). In 1999, a 5-in longer rocket motor, that utilised the space made available with the SCAS, was put into production. These improvements would be implemented into new production missiles, but the designation would remain unchanged, with Block numbers identifying modification standard. The P3I Phase III contract was awarded in November 1998 and this would introduce further improvements to the basic AMRAAM, which has a reported shelf life of 25 years. The missile has a MTBF (Mean Time Between Failure) of 1,334 hours on USAF F-15 and F-16 fighters and 888 hours on F/A-18 strike fighters.

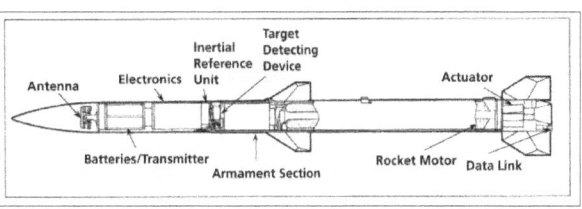

Cutaway diagram of an AIM-120 Advanced Medium Range Air to Air Missile. Raytheon

AIM-9X on the starboard wingtip station of an F/A-18F. H Harkins

When introduced to service AMRAAM was rightfully regarded as a quantum leap in capability over the AIM-7 Sparrow that it was replacing. However, while the missile has been successfully used during a number of operations and its capabilities demonstrated in numerous test firings, there has long been concern over an apparent drop-off in speed during long-range flights following rocket motor burn out. As the speed falls off the missile becomes less capable of intercepting a manoeuvring target. After launch, during rocket motor burn, AMRAAM accelerates to Mach 3, but following rocket motor burn out speed gradually decreases to between Mach 1 to Mach 1.5. The deficiencies were highlighted in January 1999, when a number of missiles were fired at Iraqi MiG's during two separate engagements, all of which failed to achieve a kill. It is thought that as speed fell off the Iraqi MiG's simply out ran the missiles.

To address the problem AMRAAM demonstrations were conducted with improved rocket motors. However, this problem, combined with the emerging threat of longer range advanced air to air missiles from Russia has seen most Western missile manufactures looking at ramjets for their respective BVR missiles. During the early 1990's, there was USAF interest in a ramjet-powered AIM-120 that would maintain the Mach 3 speed all the way to the target, providing up to four times the 'no escape zone' of comparable rocket powered missiles like the standard AMRAAM, however, the Pentagon, states it has plans to develop an extended range AIM-120.

As of 2014, AMRAAM is operated by no less than 39 nations on a variety of combat aircraft types. While being an excellent air-to-air missile AMRAAM is considered by the USN to have an inadequate engagement range for many of the BVR scenarios envisaged for the 21st century, being vastly inferior to missile in the Pan-European Meteor class.

AIM-120C-5
Propulsion: solid propellant rocket motor
Length: 3.65-m (12-ft.)
Diameter: 17.78-cm (7-inches)
Wingspan: 44.5 CM (17.5 in)
Weight: 161.5 kg (356-lb.)
Speed: Mach 3
Range: 17.38-nm (20+ miles) according to USAF data, although other data claims a range of around 40-50-km
Warhead: 20.5 kg (45 lb.) high explosive blast fragmentation
Fuzing: Proximity and contact
Guidance: active-radar
Launcher: Rail and eject

The AIM-9X program developed a short-range heat seeking weapon to be employed in both offensive and defensive counter-air operations for use by US and export nation's tactical combat aircraft as a direct AIM-9L/M replacement. The program eventually fielded a high off-boresight capable short range heat seeking missile for all three US fast jet operators and the export market.

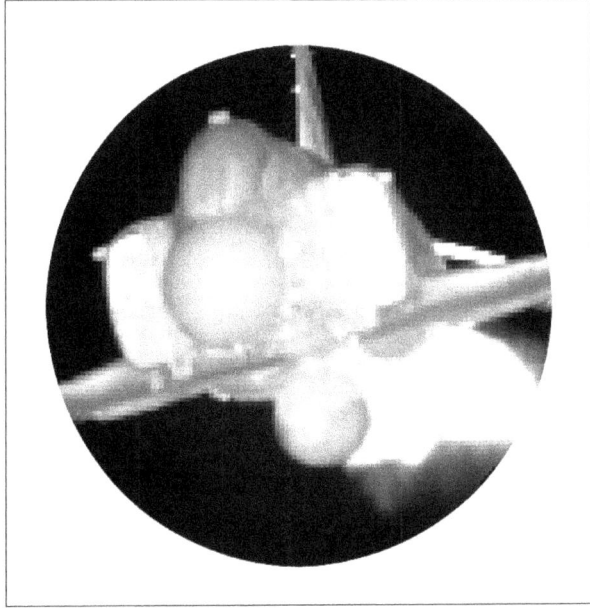

View from the seeker head of an AIM-9X development missile as it homes in on its QF-4 Phantom II target. Raytheon

The Evolved Sidewinder, also known as the Box Office 2 plus design, was developed under an USN demonstration/validation contract awarded in 1994. This weapon retained the AIM-9M's rocket motor, warhead and fuse. Using thrust-vector control increased manoeuvrability and the missile has a new IR seeker head. On 13 December 1996, the US Naval Air Systems Command selected the Hughes (now Raytheon) Evolved Sidewinder, as its preferred next generation AIM-9X close range air-to-air missile. This choice was a surprise to many observers as it was less advanced than the other main contenders put forward by Raytheon and the Hughes/BAe Dynamics ASRAAM P3I. Hughes claimed that its Evolved Sidewinder combined conformal performance with inherent growth capability in a low cost, low risk program, an argument which won through.

The new missile was required to re-establish some degree of parity of US aircraft in short range air combat, vis-à-vis improved foreign export aircraft and missile systems. Specific deficiencies existed in the AIM-9M in high off-boresight capability, infrared counter-countermeasures robustness, kinetic performance, and missile manoeuvrability. Developed variants of the Su-27/MiG-29 with their R-27 and R-73 missiles was seen as the major threat to US aircraft. Additionally, there were a number of other missiles on the world market that vastly outperformed the AIM-9M in the critical operational employment areas. The AIM-9X expanded the capabilities of the AIM-9M by incorporating a new seeker imaging infrared focal plane array, a high performance airframe, and a new signal processor for the seeker/sensor. The acquisition strategy set out to retain the warhead, fuse, and rocket motor of the AIM-9M in order to capitalise on the large existing inventory of AIM-9 weapons.

Following its selection as the AIM-9X choice Hughes (now Raytheon) received an EMD contract valued at $169 million and funding was provided for the first 1,000 missiles with up to 10,000 units then being envisaged. Initial operational capability was achieved by the USAF in November 2003, the first production rounds having been delivered to the USAF in May 2002. In USN service the missile equips the F/A-18E/F Super Hornet and F/A-18C/D Hornet while the USAF employs the weapon primarily on its F-22, F-15 and F-16 fighter aircraft; both services will field the weapon on the F-35 Lightning II.

The Super Hornet is also cleared for use with AIM-7M Sparrow semi-active radar homing and AIM-9M Sidewinder IR guided air to air missiles.

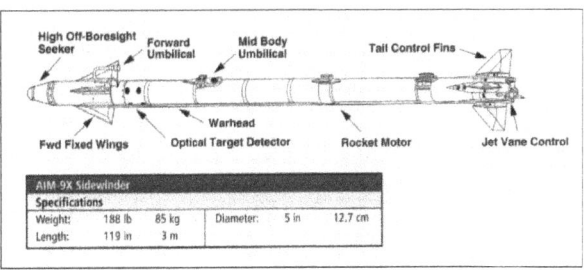

Diagram of the AIM-9X evolved Sidewinder showing the main characteristics of the weapon. Raytheon

AIM-9X

Weight: 188 lb. (85 kg)
Length: 119 in (3 m)
Diameter: 5 in (12.7 cm)
Fin Span: 17.5 in (44.45 cm)
Wing Span: 13.9 in (35.31 cm)

This F/A-18F is seen with an AGM-154A JSOW on the port inboard station, a GBU laser guided bomb on the intermediate station and an AGM-88 HARM on the outboard station. H Harkins

For the air to surface role the Super Hornet can employ precision strike and so called 'dumb' free fall iron bombs. Among legacy weapons are the Boeing AGM-84D Harpoon AShM (Anti-Ship Missile), AGM-65A Maverick ASM (Air to Surface Missile) and Boeing AGM-84E SLAM (Stand-off Land Attack Missile). Guided Bomb Units - GBU-12, 454-kg (1,000-lb.) Paveway II and GBU-16 900-kg (2,000-lb.) laser guided bombs and the full range of free fall iron bombs are also employed including the MK 82, 227-kg (500-lb.) Low Drag General Purpose (LDGP) bomb, MK 82SE 'Snakeye 227-kg (500-lb.) retarded bomb, MK 82R, 227-kg (500-lb.) bomb with BSU-86 retarded tail, MK 83 454-kg (1,000-lb.) LDGP and MK 20 Rockeye II Cluster Bomb Unit, CBU-59 and CBU-89/B 'Gator' sub-munitions dispensers. The Raytheon AGM-88 HARM (High Speed Anti-Radar Missile) is employed for SEAD (Suppression of Enemy Air Defences)

To arm the new generation of combat aircraft being developed in the US and Western Europe several new generation so called 'smart' weapons have been developed. New weapons for the Super Hornet include the Raytheon AGM-154 JSOW (Joint Stand-Off Weapon), Boeing JDAM (Joint Direct Attack Munitions), Boeing AGM-84H SLAM-ER (Stand-off Land Attack Missile-Expanded Response), Lockheed Martin AGM-158 JASSM (Joint Air to Surface Stand-off Missile) and the Raytheon AGM-88E known as the AARGM (Advanced Anti-Radar Guided Missile).

The AGM-154 JSOW, developed by Raytheon as a shorter-range complement to the SLAM ER and JASSM, has been called the 'smart truck'. The primary purpose of all the variants is to provide aircraft with the ability to strike targets from beyond most enemy air defences. The weapon started life as the AIWS (Advanced Interdiction Weapon System) being developed for the USN as a low cost replacement for the AGM-62 Walleye, AGM-123 Skipper, MK 20 Rockeye II and CBU-59 Cluster Bomb Units (CBU's), and some older generation GBU laser guided bombs.

An F/A-18C carrying a load of four JSOW's during development flight-testing of the weapon. Raytheon

In 1991, two contractors, Vought and Texas Instruments, were awarded demonstration contracts. In 1992 the USAF joined the program and the name was changed to JSOW, emphasising the joint nature of the program. Texas Instruments (now Raytheon) was selected as prime contractor the same year and development proceeded with the first guided launch of the AGM-154A variant under development for the USN taking place in 1994.

The JSOW nose section contains the GPS/INS guidance system, while the mid-body section contains the warhead and houses the high aspect ratio folding wings and the tail section houses the flight control system.

The AGM-154A, which entered service with the USN in late 1998, is the GPS/INS guided variant armed with the BLU-97 CEM (Combined Effects Munitions) or BLU-111 in the AGM-154A-1. These are effective against soft skinned vehicles, aircraft on the ground, SAM (Surface to Air Missile) sites and non-hardened targets. The AGM-154A was used operationally for the first time in January 1999, when USN F/A-18 Hornets attacked a target in Iraq.

A further variant designated AGM-154B was developed as a replacement for the AGM-65 Maverick in USN and USAF service. Another variant, the AGM-154C, armed with a BROACH blast fragmentation penetrating warhead for use against hardened targets, employing precision guidance with an IIR (Imaging InfraRed) seeker, is operated by the USN and is being integrated on RAAF (Royal Australian Air Force) F/A-18F's.

The AGM-154's pop-out wings allow a range from a high altitude (40,000 ft.) launch of around 130 km (70 nm) and 22 km (15 nm) for a launch at 500 ft. altitude, un-powered.

An AGM-154A JSOW with wings extended. H Harkins

Among the main offensive weapons employed by the Super Hornet is the Boeing GBU-29/30 JDAM, which is basically a 454-kg (1,000-lb.) or 907-kg (2,000-lb.) conventional iron bomb fitted with a tail-kit housing a GPS/INS guidance system for the body kit, and a 1760A weapons interface, producing the GBU-29, 907-kg and GBU-30, 454-kg respectively. The baseline weapon was the 900-kg weapon, which can have either the MK 84 blast-fragmentation or the BLU-109 target penetration warheads. The smaller GBU-29 454-kg JDAM variant was developed for internal carriage in the Lockheed/Boeing F-22 as the larger weapon will not fit in the internal weapons bay. Development of the GBU-30 454-kg weapon ran around one year behind the larger 900-kg weapon. Further variants of JDAM including kits for incorporation on 227-kg (500-lb) weapons were also developed.

During a conventional iron bomb attack the weapon system computer on the launch aircraft takes a number of factors into account such as wind velocity and altitude and computes the weapons trajectory to position the aircraft at the ideal release point. With JDAM things are taken a step further. The target co-ordinates are programmed into the JDAM while on the ground, although these can be changed in flight, allowing alternative targets to be attacked.

During the mission planning the pilot can select impact angles of between 10° and 30°. According to Boeing the flight path to the target can also be programmed into the weapon allowing it to fly around the target, for example a building, and attack it from the side.

Flight testing of JDAM began at Eglin AFB, Florida, in October 1996, demonstrating better than the 13 m (40 ft.) required by the customers. JDAM entered full operational service with the USAF in 1998 and the weapon made its combat debut on 24 March 1999, during operation Allied Force, the NATO air attacks on the Federal Republic of Yugoslavia. During this attack 32 x 908-kg (2,000-lb.) JDAM's were dropped on the first mission, 16 each from the two Northrop Grumman B-2 'Spirit' stealth bombers. During the course of the campaign the B-2A force dropped in excess of 600 JDAM's.

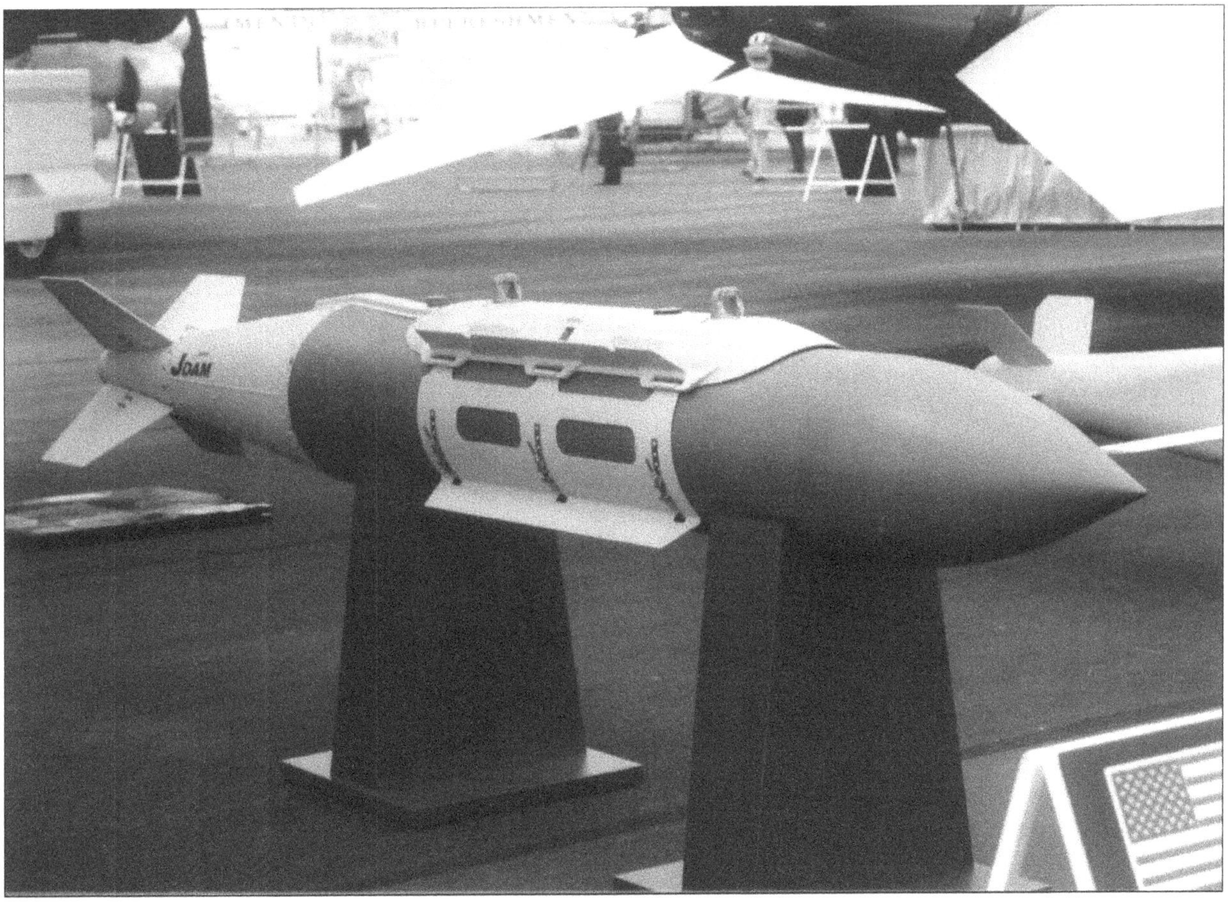
JDAM

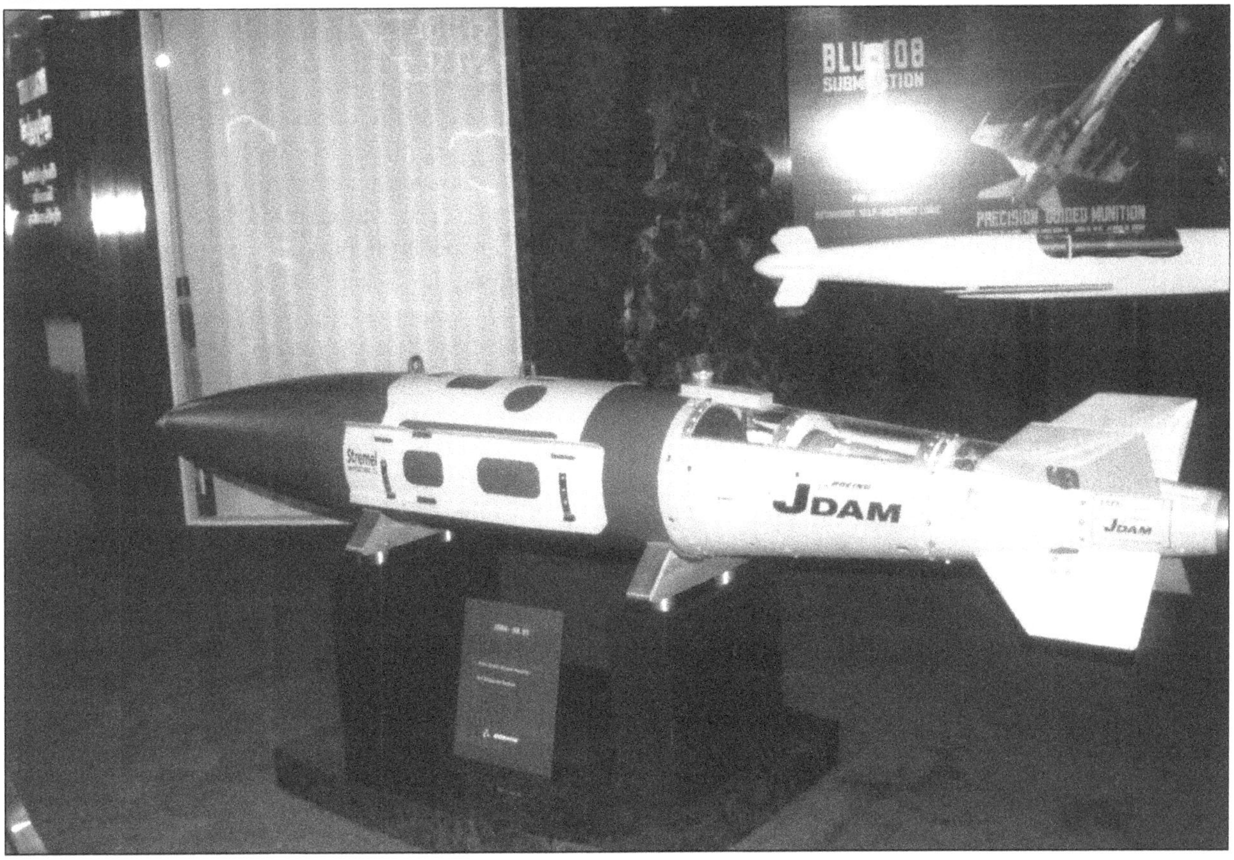
PRECISION GUIDED MUNITION
Stremel
BOEING
JDAM
JDAM

Previous page: Boeing JDAM. H Harkins **Above: An AGM-84E SLAM model at Farnborough in 1996. The transparent area shows the imaging infrared seeker, which replaced the radar seeker of the AGM-84D Harpoon.** H Harkins

By the late 1980's it was becoming obvious that delays were going to seriously delay the AGM-137 TSSAM (Tri-Service Stand-off Attack Missile), planned for the USAF/USN/USMC, introduction to service. As a stopgap solution to equip the USN with a credible standoff air to surface missile capability, McDonnell Douglas offered the AGM-84E SLAM (Standoff Land Attack Missile) which was derived from the AGM-84D Harpoon anti-ship missile.

The SLAM program began in 1989, and development was swift, enabling the weapon to be used operationally during the 1991 Gulf war with Iraq, when an USN A-6E Intruder strike aircraft successfully launched a pair of missiles at an Iraqi hydroelectric plant.

SLAM is basically a Harpoon missile body with the radar seeker replaced by the imaging infrared seeker of the AGM-65D Maverick, combined with an integrated GPS/INS and the data-link pod of the AGM-62 Walleye glide bomb. Once released by the launch aircraft the missile flies autonomously until it nears the target area. The data-link and the seeker are then automatically activated, allowing images of the target to be transmitted to the launch aircraft or third party, an operator then selects an aim point before locking on the seeker.

In December 1994, both the USN and USAF cancelled the TSSAM, placing greater importance on SLAM, the potential of which spurred further development of its stand-off capabilities, to provide improvements in range, accuracy, warhead penetration, dive angle and mission planning. Due in part to the USN's growing focus on littoral warfare, the SLAM ER (Expanded Response) program initiatives were formalised in December 1994, when the Assistant Secretary of the Navy for Research, Development and Acquisition gave the go ahead to proceed with engineering and manufacturing development and accelerate SLAM ER production and deployment to the fleet. The USN contracted MDC to develop an improved variant of the SLAM missile designated AGM-84H, known as SLAM ER.

An F/A-18C from the NAWC-WD with a SLAM ER on the Port inboard wing station during a live fire test in 1999. SLAM ER has now entered full-scale production and operational service with the F/A-18C/D. Boeing

The AGM-84H, which evolved into the AGM-84K, is an evolutionary upgrade of SLAM featuring day/night, adverse weather, over-the-horizon and precision strike capability. This variant, which began to bend the AGM-84 design out of shape, included a revised nose which reduces drag as well as being more 'stealthy', and introduced larger folding planer wings which extend the range of the missile by 50% to 100% over that of the SLAM depending on launch altitude; range being around 150-nautical miles. The missile, which is 172 in in length and has a diameter of 13.5 in, has an improved warhead to increase penetration and lethality against hardened targets, and software improvements that make it easier for the control aircraft to designate track on the target aim point.

Significant enhancement are: a highly accurate, GPS-aided guidance system; improved missile aerodynamic performance characteristics that allow both greater range and more- effective terminal attack profiles; a redesigned ordnance section for increased penetrating power and lethality; and a more user-friendly interface for both Man-in-the-Loop control and mission planning. SLAM-ER was the first weapon to feature ATA (Automatic Target Acquisition), a revolutionary technological breakthrough, which automates and improves target acquisition in cluttered scenes and can overcome most countermeasures and environmentally degraded conditions. Other features of the SLAM-ER include the Harris/Magnavox Improved Data-link, which has both increased range and increased resistance to jamming. While the missile is in flight, the GPS receiver/processor updates the missile's inertial navigation system helping to ensure that the imaging infrared seeker is pointed directly at the target.

The new nose section houses the improved warhead, a 500-lb derivative of the Tomahawk Block III warhead developed by the Naval Air Warfare Centre Weapons Division at China Lake. The titanium WDU-40/B warhead is shaped specifically to increase penetration and becomes reactive during detonation, substantially increasing the blast and incendiary effects.

An AGM-84H SLAM ER at Farnborough 2000. This view shows to advantage the large size of the extended planner wings in comparison to the missile body. H Harkins

The man-in-the-loop feature allows the pilot to precisely update the point of impact during the missiles final moments of flight. The data-link in the missile is used to transmit an image of the target to the controlling aircraft. A key feature of the SLAM ER's improved man-in-the-loop interface, known as the Stop-Motion Aim point Update, allows the control aircraft pilot to freeze the target scene video on the cockpit display, designate a precise aim point and then command the missile to attack that specific aim point. This guidance mode allows the missile to attack and hit critical aim points even when the aim points have no distinguishing infrared signature.

The man-in-the-loop control system offers several tactically significant advantages over other types of standoff weapon guidance systems. Viewing the target scene in real time prior to impact allows target identification, reduced possibility of so called 'collateral damage', selection of a secondary aim point in the event the original target has already been destroyed, and an immediate indication of mission effectiveness. The Boeing developed Automatic Target Acquisition System will provides even greater capability for SLAM ER.

SLAM ER entered full production in June 2000 following completion of an operational evaluation and small numbers were employed in the invasions of Iraq and Afghanistan in the early 2000's.

A Boeing AGM-84H SLAM ER during a 1999 test launch. Boeing

The AGM-88 HARM on the port outer wing station of an F/A-18F. H Harkins

SLAM ER

Length: 436.9-cm (172-in; 14-ft. 4-in).
Diameter: 34.29-cm (13.5-in)
Wing Span: 2-m 18.2-cm (85.9-in; 7.158-ft.)
Weight: 668.1-kg (1,473-lb.)
Range: 150-nm+ (277.95-km+)
Speed: high subsonic
Propulsion: Teledyne Turbojet and solid propellant booster for surface and submarine launch with thrust greater than 600-lb (greater than 272.16 kg). Only the air launched variant is currently in service.
Guidance: ring laser gyro Inertial Navigation System (INS) with multi-channel GPS (Global Positioning System); infrared seeker for terminal guidance with Man-in-the-Loop control data-link from the controlling aircraft. Upgraded missiles will incorporate Automatic Target Acquisition
Date Deployed: 2000

The Lockheed Martin AGM-158 JASSM (Joint Air to Surface Standoff Missile), selected for production in 1998, was developed for the USAF and USN as a long-range stand-off precision strike weapon. The USN, however, does not operate the weapon, which is certified for use on RAAF Super Hornets, although not employed.

One of the primary weapons for the Super Hornet is the Raytheon AGM-88 HARM. This weapon has been used operationally in a number of conflicts, with mixed results, employed by the USN and USAF, both services embarking upon a program to improve their respective HARM capabilities with the adoption of the improved AGM-88C, which features a more sensitive seeker-head, additional on-board memory and improved processors. The capability of the AGM-88C is further enhanced with the introduction of the HARM Block V software which continued the evolution of the HARM system, giving the missile capability to attack not only air defence radar systems, but jamming systems also.

At Farnborough in July 2000, the AARGM appeared to have metamorphosed into what appeared to be an improved HARM. The similarity to which can be seen in the model.
H Harkins

At the 42nd Paris air salon in June 1997, two contenders to replace the Raytheon AGM-88-HARM in USN/USAF service were unveiled. This emerged as the AARGM (Advanced Anti-Radiation Guided Missile) program which at first looked at all-new missile systems, but later settled on an evolutionary upgrade of the AGM-88C, designated AGM-88E, which features a GPS/INS guidance, net centric connectivity, a digital anti-radiation homing sensor, a MMW (Millimetric Wave) radar and impact assessment. The AGM-88E entered full rate production in August 2012 and initial operational capability was expected in late summer 2014

A further evolution of the AGM-88 led to the AGM-88F, which was test launched in August 2014. This variant features an HCSM (HARM Control Section Modification), which "is more precise and accurate… with GPS/IMU navigation accuracy, giving HARM the ability to engage time critical targets."

The two-seat F/A-18F operational conversion trainer is fully combat capable with only a slight reduction in combat radius over the single-seat F/A-18E. While it is capable of carrying all the weapons carried by the single-seat 'E' model it may be armed with rockets to designate targets in the fast FAC (Forward Air Controller) role. The standard 12.7-cm (5-in) Zuni rocket is to be replaced by a new weapon.

The only fixed armament is the internal nose mounted 20-mm M61A1 six barrelled cannon which can be used in the air to air and air to ground role. This weapon is the same as that fitted to the F/A-18C/D and a number of other US and foreign built fighter aircraft, being capable of firing at a rate of up to 6,000 rounds per minute, with a muzzle velocity of 1036 m (3,400 ft.) per second. The Super Hornet retains the same 570 round capacity as the F/A-18C/D.

F/A-18F2 is seen in this three photograph sequence launching the first of two AGM-88 HARM missiles in the first duel shot HARM firing at the NAWC-WD, China Lake ranges on 3 December 1998. NAWC-WD

Top: This aircraft is loaded with three drop tanks on the centreline and the two inboard wing stations, 2,000-lb. bombs on the intermediate wing stations, AGM-88 HARM's on the outboard wing stations and AIM-9M's on the wingtip stations. Boeing
Above: An F/A-18F launches an AGM-88E AARGM. NAVAIR

Chapter 4

SUPER HORNET ENGINEERING & MANUFACURING DEVELOPMENT PHASE

An underside view of F/A-18E1, the first Super Hornet prototype, during an early test flight out of St Louis, Missouri. Boeing

The EMD contract, signed on 7 December 1992, was to run for seven and a half years and included the building of eight (later reduced to seven) flight test prototypes consisting of five single-seat F/A-18E and three (later reduced to two) two-seat F/A-18F's, along with three ground test airframes, the latter being delivered by 1997. In addition, various F/A-18E models were used to test the radar cross section of the aircraft. In 1995, MDC hoisted a full-scale model of F/A-18E onto a 42 ft. test tower at Smart Field, St Charles, Missouri. This model was used for antenna testing and is scheduled to remain in use throughout the aircraft's life.

As well as the seven prototypes a number of other aircraft were involved in the development program, including a number of F/A-18C/D's, one such aircraft being F/A-18D BuNo164649/114 from the Naval Air Warfare Centre WD (Weapons Division) based at NAS (Naval Air Station) China Lake, California, which was primarily used as an avionics test-bed; the aircraft being adorned with E/F, Avionics Test Be lettering on the vertical tail fins.

The flight development program was conducted primarily at NAS Patuxent River, Maryland on Eastern Coast of the United States. This facility being the USN's premier flight test and evaluation establishment, graced with extensive technical and range facilities.

The second Super Hornet prototype, F/A-18E2, made its first flight from St Louis on 26 December 1995. Boeing

Unlike previous aircraft programs, the Super Hornet program was conducted under the aegis of an Integrated Test Team (ITT) which consisted of the USN, Boeing (formerly McDonnell Douglas), Northrop Grumman, General Electric and Hughes (now Raytheon). The ITT was a new concept and the resultant close co-operation of the entire team throughout the test program allowed all team members access to all parameters of the test program and to provide input at all stages.

The ITT was able to use Patuxent Rivers on site telemetry systems, allowing the designers, engineers and other program personnel to view real time data transmitted direct from the test aircraft onto the consoles at the ground stations, allowing them to closely monitor the various readings. The team also had access to other bases and Super Hornets were based at Edward's AFB, California, as required for cross-wind landing tests, and Naval Air Facility (NAF), Lakehurst, for carrier suitability tests and catapult launches. Each aircraft was already equipped for its specific testing tasks prior to delivery to 'Pax River'. E5 and F2 were equipped to what was closest to the production standard aircraft, being used as weapons systems test aircraft.

The Super Hornet EMD program came under the control of the Strike Test Directorate. Of the ten test pilots originally working on the Super Hornet program, five were from the USN, four from Boeing and one from Northrop Grumman.

Air to air refuelling allowed longer flights to be conducted and the ITT utilised the Lockheed Martin KC-130 tankers of the Strike Test Squadron for this purpose. On all test flights the Super Hornets were accompanied by chase aircraft, mostly other Hornets, supplied by the Strike Test squadron.

The third prototype single-seat Super Hornet F/A-18E3 was the last of the proto2 types to be delivered to the ITT arriving at Patuxent River on 2 February 1997. Boeing

MDC unveiled the first prototype, F/A-18E1, (BuNo165164), at St Louis, Missouri, on 18 September 1995. At the roll-out ceremony the Chief of Naval Operations, Admiral Jeremy Boorda, revealed that the F/A-18E/F had been officially named 'Super Hornet'.

At the roll-out, E1 demonstrated the Super Hornet's versatility as it was carrying six different underwing weapon options: the AGM-88 HARM; AGM-84D Harpoon AShM; AGM-84H SLAM-ER ASM; GBU-29 JDAM; AGM-154 JSOW and AGM-65E Maverick air to surface missile. In addition AIM-9 Sidewinder short-range air to air missiles were carried on the wingtip stations, a single AMRAAM was carried on the starboard side fuselage station and an AN/AAS-46 targeting FLIR was carried on the port side fuselage station. E1 had the markings of VFA-131 'Wildcats' adorning its starboard tail fin and the markings of VFA-142 on the port tail fin.

Following the formalities of the official roll-out, MDC concentrated on getting E1 ready for its first flight, then scheduled for 31 November 1995, not being coy about announcing that prior to the first flight the development program was on time and on budget and the basic aircraft was some 450 kg below the specification weight required by the customer.

Prior to the first flight MDC completed a series of ground runs of the F414 turbofans, including afterburning trials, along with high-speed taxi tests at St Louis. The first flight from St Louis Lambert International Airport was two days ahead of schedule when F/A-18E1 took-off at 11.55 hours on 29 November 1995, with MDC Chief Test Pilot Fred Maidenwald at the controls. The flight, which lasted 20 minutes, was cut short when an environmental control-system warning light illuminated in the cockpit, showing an environmental control system bleed door failure, but the aircraft "...was smooth, precise and easy to control" stated Maidenwald who also added, the design goal of providing handling "as good as or better than that of the F/A-18C/D" had been achieved. At the end of the flight the aircraft landed with some 4500 kg of fuel remaining, which was "... more than the 'C/D' takes off with". The aircraft touched down at a speed of 132 knots (254 km/h) while the F/A-18D chase aircraft landed at a speed of 146 knots, demonstrating the 'E/F's' slower landing speed.

The first two-seat prototype F/A-18F1 made its first flight on April fools day 1996. Here the aircraft is about to take the wire during initial carrier qualifications aboard the USS John C Stennis in January 1997. Boeing

MDC hoped to fly the second aircraft, F/A-18E2, (BuNo165165), by 16 December 1995, but this was delayed until 26 December.

Following an initial series of check-out flights at St Louis, MDC was due to deliver the first two aircraft, E1 and E2, to the Naval Air Warfare Centre-Aircraft Division (NAWC-AD) at Patuxent River, in January 1996. However, the first aircraft, E1, didn't arrive at Patuxent River until 14 February 1996, beginning a three year, 2,000 sortie, and 3,000-hour flight test program. By this time E1 had completed 6 flights in 8.8 hours from St Louis and the second aircraft, E2, had completed four flights in 5.6 hours.

The EMD flight test program was scheduled for completion by December 1998, but ran on until spring 1999. It was estimated that each aircraft would conduct around ten sorties per month with each sortie averaging around 1.4 hours in the air, although the ITT confirmed that the aircraft were flying significantly more than this.

The first task of the ITT was to clear the aircraft for air to air refuelling, allowing extended missions covering several separate tasks to be flown in a single sortie. The second prototype, E2, made its 5th flight on 17 February 1996, and was delivered to Patuxent River two days later. F/A-18E1 was to be used for envelope expansion while E2 was allocated for propulsion performance testing.

A development program milestone occurred on 1 April 1996, when the first two-seat Super Hornet, F/A-18F1, (BuNo165166), made its first flight from St Louis. The following day E1 performed the first supersonic flight, attaining Mach 1.1 and an altitude of 48,000 ft. during the course of a three-hour sortie over the North Atlantic. On the 3rd of the month the speed envelope was pushed to Mach 1.52. Amid the excitement of these achievement's the mood of the Integrated Test Team at Patuxent River was blackened by reports in the US press that the Super Hornet program could be cancelled following the leaking of a controversial General Accounting Office report which severely criticised the program, claiming that it offered only marginal improvements over the existing 'C/D' variant of the Hornet and suggested upgraded variants of the F/A-18C/D should be purchased as the USN awaited the Joint Strike Fighter.

Previous page: This overhead view of F/A-18E1 in formation with an F/A-18C Hornet clearly illustrates the increase in overall dimensions of the larger Super Hornet. Boeing

Above: F/A-18E4 made its first flight on 2 July 1996 and was delivered to Patuxent River on 22 August that year. It is here being refuelled by F/A-18E1 over the Atlantic Ocean on 11 March 1999. Boeing

Amid the political jostling, the test team continued with the program which was running smoothly, reaching 100 flight hours on 14 May 1996. F/A-18F1 was allocated to carrier suitability testing and was delivered to the ITT at Patuxent River, arriving at 18.46 hours on 21 May 1996 following a 2 hour 36 minute delivery flight from St Louis. By 23 May the three aircraft, E1, E2 and F1, had flown 78 sorties in 129.7 hours, with the longest sortie of five hours being conducted by E2 on 22 May.

On 11 June 1996, all three of the then current flying aircraft were for the first time airborne at the same time above Maryland at around 4.00 pm. The pilots involved were MDC lead test pilot Fred Maidenwald flying E1, Northrop Grumman test pilot Jim Sandberg flying E2 and USN Lieutenant Frank Morely flying F1. By 12 June, E1 had accumulated 43 flights, E2, 46 flights and F1, 10 flights, for a total of 99 flights in 169.5 hours. The following day the 100-flight milestone was reached and by the 26th, 200 flight hours had been attained.

In mid-1996, Lt Com Gurney stated that his initial impression of the F/A-18E/F was that "the performance is better than the current 'C/D' models. The 'E/F' gives the ability to climb faster, manoeuvre better at high altitudes, and has more endurance" MDC stated that the 'E/F' handling qualities were "far superior" to those of the 'C/D' due to its larger size and larger control surfaces.

The fourth prototype, F/A-18E4, (BuNo165168), conducted a 1.6-hour maiden flight from St Louis on 2 July 1996. By 8 July, E1 had accumulated 53 flights in 88.6 flight hours, E2, 56 flights in 110.3 flight hours, F1, 13 flights in 22.9 flight hours and E4, 1 flight in 1.6 flight hours, for a total of 126 flights in 217.9 flight hours.

F/A-18F1's test program began to gather pace when the aircraft conducted the first steam-ingestion catapult tests on 5 August 1996. The aircraft completed three launches from a land-based steam-catapult at Patuxent River. The first arrested landings were completed by F1 at NAF Lakehurst, Virginia, on 21 August 1996. The following day, F/A-18E4 was delivered to the ITT at Patuxent River following a 2.2-hour ferry flight from St Louis, by which time the flight test program had reached 300 flight hours.

E4 was primarily involved in high AoA (Angle of Attack) flight-testing. Unlike the three earlier aircraft E1, E2 and F1, which were painted in a mid-sea grey colour scheme, E4 was painted in a high visibility white and orange colour scheme to aid ground tracking cameras. E4 was also fitted with a spin chute mounted between the two vertical tails for spin tests.

August also saw the first flight of the fifth prototype, F/A-18E5, BuNo.164169, when this aircraft conducted a two hour flight on the 27th, by which time around 171 flights in 300 flight-hours had been accumulated with 400 flight hours being passed in September.

E5 was the first of two avionics and weapons systems aircraft, the other being F/A-18F2, BuNo164170, which conducted its first flight on 11 October 1996. This was the sixth Super Hornet to fly, and, together with E5, was used to validate weapon separation and missile system performance.

During the development program the F414 engine was to undergo 13,000 hours running on the ground and in the air using 32 development engines. By August 1996 the F414 had accumulated some 650 hours running in the F/A-18E/F, and General Electric claimed that the engine portion of the flight test program was 90% complete. The engine development program had some problems to overcome, however, such as the discovery of a 15Hz oscillation in the fuel system, alterations being made to the flow body of the engine. This translated into "...dynamic discharges that could be felt in the cockpit and which affected engine performance." The early test engines produced "...significant exhaust smoke, which is not a good thing." This problem was solved by hardware modifications to the combustor. A nozzle control issue was cured by software modifications to the F414s Full-Authority Digital Engine Control system.

The USN planned to purchase some 2,300 F414 engines, however with the reduction in Super Hornet numbers the number of engines to be purchased was also significantly reduced.

Top: F/A-18E5, the last of the single-seat prototypes, conducted its maiden flight from St Louis on 27 August 1996. The aircraft is here arriving at NAS China Lake, California, in 1998. Above: F/A-18E5, foreground, in formation with the F/A-18F2 over NAS China Lake in 1998. Both E5 and F2 were fitted out as avionics and weapon-system prototypes. NAWC-WD

During late 1996, the ITT reported unexpected problems in its evaluation of the aircraft. The problems included a "distinct wing-drop tendency" when accelerating through 13° to 15° AoA. The wing-drop was rectified by modifying the control scheduling of a vent in the aircraft's large LERX's (Leading Edge Root Extensions), which are 34% larger than those of the 'C/D', to improve pitch control at high AoA, and incorporate a vent, which allows high-energy air to flow over the wing-fuselage blend. Analysis conducted by the team revealed significant flow separation over the outer wing panel with "asymmetric bursts" causing the sudden wing drop, the LERX vents them 'up' for all power approach configurations.

The last Super Hornet prototype to fly was the second two-seater, F/A-18F2, which conducted its maiden flight on 11 October 1996. It is here on arrival at China Lake on 3 April 1998. The aircraft was based at China Lake for weapons development testing with the F-18 AWL. NAWC-WD

The evaluation also revealed aileron limit-cycle oscillation, originally generated by flutter excitation. The team studied various cures for this aero-elastic condition, including changing the aileron bias in the neutral position, and stiffening up the structure of the aileron shroud.

In October 1996, the program was awarded the Aircraft Design award from the American Institute of Aeronautics and Astronautics. However, the celebrations were cut short in, November, when the almost trouble free flight test program ran into its first real problem when a General Electric F414-400 engine suffered a compressor stall during supersonic flight testing which resulted in internal damage. The pilot was able to retard the engine to idle and return to base. The flight test program was immediately suspended pending an investigation, which included the removal and inspection of all the remaining flight engines. During the grounding General Electric developed a fix for the fault, described as a cracked compressor blade, and MDC stated that the Super Hornet development schedule was unaffected as the company completed the planned wing modifications during the grounding. To enable the impending CarQuals (Carrier Qualifications) to proceed, General Electric fixed the two engines for F1 and an-additional two engines held as spares on the aircraft carrier USS *John C. Stennis*, at the time the latest *Nimitz* class carrier, which commissioned in 1995. During February 1997, the remaining aircraft had the modified engines installed.

Originally scheduled for November 1996, the initial CarQuals were rescheduled for January 1997, and commenced on the 18th of the month when F/A-18F1, piloted by USN Lt Frank Morley, made the first arrested landing aboard the USS *John C Stennis*. On its initial landing F1 took the number three wire.

F/A-18F1 conducted the Super Hornet programs first carrier landing on 18 January 1997. Boeing **Below: F1 touches down and takes the wire on 18 January 1997.** USN

During the course of the next five days F1 conducted 64 arrested landings and launches and 54 touch and goes. The sea trials demonstrated a landing speed of 135 knots (250-km/h) which is a 10-knot reduction in approach speed compared with the F/A-18C/D. Other tests included single-engine, cross wind and failure-mode approaches, all of which were apparently successful.

The first Super Hornet carrier landing was conducted by USN Lt Frank Morely, while Lt Commander Tom Gurney made the first Super Hornet carrier take-off. Of the flying qualities in the landing pattern, Gurney commented that they are "much better". Adding "it's a little more stable because its heavier and has more wing area, increased efficiency and manoeuvrability at high altitudes and offers reduced approach speed." A second series of sea trials was scheduled for 1998, but delayed until spring 1999, and two early operational assessments of the aircraft were conducted in 1997-98.

Following the sea trials F1 returned to Patuxent River on 23 January to begin preparations for weapons testing. The previous day had seen the delivery of the second F/A-18F, F2, to the ITT at Patuxent River. At this time MDC revealed that the Super Hornet was one third of the way through the flight test program, which despite the November setback remained on schedule and on budget. The last of the seven development Super Hornet's was delivered to Patuxent River when E3 arrived there on 1 February 1997. At that time the seven Super Hornets had accumulated 390 sorties in 630.9 flight hours. E3 was primarily used for loads testing.

The stores separation phase, conducted at Patuxent River, involved the release of single, paired, multiple and ripple stores configurations. The Super

F/A-18F1 about to conduct the first carrier catapult launch during initial sea trials in January 1997. USN

Hornet program saw the evaluation and loading of more types of stores than had ever been conducted that early in an aircraft's development, Patuxent River being ideally located for weapons separation tests with inland and off-coast ranges available. During the weapons separation tests more than 50 types of stores were released to evaluate late changes to the stores pylons following the prediction during wind tunnel tests of collisions of adjacent stores on the inboard pylons.

The stores separation test phase commenced on 19 February 1997 when E5 dropped an empty 1,820 litre (480 gal.) centreline mounted fuel tank from an altitude of 5,000 ft. Two day E1 flew with a stores configuration of three 480 gallon fuel tanks, one on the centreline and one on each of the inboard wing stations, a MK 84 bomb on each of the intermediate wing stations; two AGM-88's on the outer wing stations and a pair of AIM-9 Sidewinders on the wingtip stations. This flight commenced at a take-off weight of 28300-kg (62,260-lb.) which was the heaviest take-off weight attempted by a Super Hornet at that time.

By late March 1997, the test fleet had accumulated over 700 hours in around 450 sorties. The external stores testing phase had included airborne release of external fuel tanks from stations 4, 6 and 8, MK 82, 83, 84 and CBU-100 bombs, and AGM-84D, and AGM-84E missiles. Highlights of the month included the airdrop of a stick of MK 82 bombs on the 13th, and the release of a Harpoon and a SLAM missile on the 17th and 18th respectively. ALE-47 and ALE-50 defensive countermeasures were also launched during this phase. By the end of the month about 85% of the flight envelope had been cleared and it was revealed that no flight control changes were necessary from the initial sea trial data.

On 3 April 1997 all seven development aircraft flew on the same day (some of them three times), for the first time in the program, for a total of 13 sorties. Two days later, the 5th, E5 fired the first missile of the test program, an AIM-9 Sidewinder, with another Sidewinder being launched from the same aircraft on the 9th. On both occasions the weapon was launched from the starboard wingtip station, an AMRAAM also being launched on the 5th.

The second two-seat prototype, F/A-18F2, background is seen in formation with an F/A-18D Hornet of the Strike Aircraft Test Squadron over Chesopeeke Bay. USN

On 8 April, E1 pushed the flight envelope to Mach 1.65 and later extended this to Mach 1.73 in clean configuration. By the end of April over 593 sorties had been flown in over 937 flight-hours. On 13 May the 1000 flight hour milestone was reached.

From April 1998 F/A-18F2 was transferred to NAS China Lake, California, for testing, including software development and verification.

Once the initial flight test program was completed all seven test aircraft were based between Patuxent River and China Lake, being available for on-going weapons and avionics development tests. VX-9, based at China Lake, headed the Super Hornet tactics and operational doctrine (effectively writing the operational manuals).

The mood of the ITT was best summed-up by the people associated with the program. The Government Flight Test Director, Commander Robert Wirt, said, "It (the Super Hornet) flies like a 'C/D', but better. Our pilots have given it very good marks for longitudinal and lateral directional handling, both up and away, as well as in the landing pattern. In addition engine response has been excellent." Commenting on the 'E/F's' handling qualities, Commander. Wirt said "The aircraft is a little bit bigger, therefore, it has a lot better gust response, and is a lot more stable in the 'up-and-away' configuration and during landing". In defence of the F/A-18E/F he said, "We are now out of growth capability on the 'C/D'." Boeings Fred Maidenwald said that the high AoA has been improved over the C/D, and control laws in the FBW FCS system have been modified, reducing side-slip and improving roll rates at high AoA. He went on to say that the F/A-18E/F would be fully manoeuvrable beyond 40° AoA instead of the 35° AoA of the F/A-18C/D.

The ITT stated "The aircraft is clearly superior [to the 'C/D' in subsonic acceleration and climb. The jury is still out in the transonic and supersonic acceleration areas, although the requirement was that the F/A-18E/F should be as good as or better than the F/A-18C/D", and it appears that in most respects the latter will be the case.

The Super Hornet soared through the 1,500 flight-hour at 11 a.m. on 29 August. At the controls of E1 was ITT pilot Jim Sandberg, of Northrop Grumman.

An uninhabited Super Hornet ground-test article was used for barrier testing at NAS Lakehurst, New Jersey. Barrier testing began in September 1997 and was completed in November that year. NAWC-WD

By 3 September 1997, the test team had flown a total of 970 flights and the 1,000th flight milestone was reached on the 12th of the month, with Commander. Rob Niewoehner at the controls. Earlier that day, ITT pilots flew seven flights, setting the stage for the one hour duration 1,000th flight. The 2,000-flight hour milestone was passed on 9 December 1997; F/A-18F2, taking off 10:02 a.m. on a 1.8 hours sortie during which an AIM-120A was launched at the edges of the flight envelope. At the end of the day, during which six of the Super Hornets completed nine flights, the flight test program totals were 1,308 flights and 2,003.1 flight-hours.

In summary, during 1997 the Super Hornet fleet underwent a variety of flight tests, including high AoA and spin tests; flying qualities and performance tests; weapon delivery/accuracy tests; weapon separation tests; launch of air-to-air missiles, including AIM-9 Sidewinder, AIM-7 Sparrow and AIM-120 AMRAAM air to air missiles as well as the release of air-to-ground weapons (Harpoon, SLAM, GBU-10, HARM and Maverick); and release of free-fall air to ground stores, MK 76, BDU-48, Mk-82LD, Mk-83HD and Mk-84) iron bombs.

Three ground test articles conducted barrier and drop tests and underwent static and fatigue testing, and live-fire testing was conducted at China Lake. The barrier test phase commenced in early September 1997. Propelled by a special jet "car", an uninhabited F/A-18E streaked down a track at speeds comparable to those of an aircraft landing on an aircraft carrier deck. Instead of using a tail-hook to catch an arresting cable, the Super Hornet was stopped safely by a nylon barricade. This was the first of six tests at NAS Lakehurst, New Jersey, to demonstrate the Super Hornet's compatibility with the emergency barricades employed on aircraft carriers, stretched across the carrier deck, as an emergency measure to stop the aircraft. The test F/A-18E accelerated to 110.8 knots over a 6,000-ft run, engaged the barricade and came to rest approximately after 200 yards. Upon completion of the barricade engagement test phase in November 1997, the F/A-18E ground test vehicle was returned to St. Louis for refurbishment in preparation for a series of live-fire testing.

F/A-18F2 launches a Raytheon AIM-9 Sidewinder during weapons separation testing. USN

In August 1998, the F/A-18E/F successfully reached another development milestone when the full-scale fatigue test airframe (FT50) completed its first lifetime of testing in the Boeing St. Louis laboratories (Boeing having taken over McDonnell Douglas Corporation in 1997). One lifetime of fatigue testing is the equivalent of 6,000 flight hours, or about 20 years of operational use. FT50 was a structurally complete airframe, minus the internal subsystems. It was built to demonstrate the strength and durability of the Super Hornet. Fatigue testing simulates the variety of conditions that the Super Hornet would be exposed to during operational flying - everything from flight manoeuvres to carrier-landings. To simulate these conditions 176 hydraulic actuators applied 2.69 million load variations to the airframe during the course of testing. The FT50 team collected continuous data from more than 1,500 data channels.

Fatigue cycling on FT50 commenced on 30 June 1997, and reached the one-lifetime milestone one month earlier than scheduled. During tests laboratory engineers increased the fatigue cycling rate, which reduced total cycling time, and offset down times for FT50 configuration updates and unplanned repairs. Completion of the first lifetime was an exit criterion for USN Program Review III, which was conducted in November 1998. Full funding for the third lot of low-rate initial production aircraft was contingent on the successful completion of this program review.

Fatigue testing provides design engineers with critical information used to determine the likelihood and causes of premature fatigue damage or wear on the aircraft's structural components. A comprehensive inspection of FT50 was completed, and the first lifetime test data analysed.

F2 launches a Raytheon AIM-120 AMRAAM during weapons separation testing. The first AMRAAM was launched from F2 on 5 May 1997. USN

F/A-18F2 taxis at NAS China Lake following its delivery flight on 3 April 1998. NAWC-WD

During flight testing, a wing drop problem that produced abrupt unexpected buffeting when manoeuvring hard at high subsonic speed was encountered. Boeing looked at a number of possible solutions, including software and aerodynamic approaches, including an 18-in inboard extension of the dog-toothed outer wing panels and leading-edge flaps, six small strips above the wings, grit tape and a porous chord-wise fairing over the central wing fold. The last mentioned being favoured, along with software changes. Variable porosity to the airflow in the wing fold-fairing blister was achieved by drilling small holes in its forward's section, increasing in diameter toward the rear. These affectedly rendered the fairing transparent to the airflow and eliminated un-commanded bank angles from asymmetric wing-lift as well as reducing buffet to a minimum.

Some problems were also experienced with the cable of the interim ALE-50 towed decoy when operating in afterburner. However, it was expected that the problem would be minimised once the fibre-optic cable of the definitive ALE-50 was deployed.

F/A-18F2 was joined at China Lake by F/A-18E5 on 22 April 1998. Here both aircraft take-off from China Lake. Both F/A-18F2, background, and F/A-18E5, foreground, were involved in avionics and weapon-system development. NAWC-WD

F/A-18E2 poses for the camera with a load of AIM-9 Sidewinder, AGM-88 HARM, 2,000-lb bombs and external fuel tanks. Boeing

On 1 July 1998, the program passed 3,000 flight hours, during which the aircraft completed the requirements for the basic flight envelope, conducted more than 1,400 aerial refuelling and completed initial carrier qualifications and cross-wind landings. Weapons configuration flights had been initiated on all 26 different configurations to be tested. Weapons separation tests included the firing of 25 missiles and dropping of more than 430,000 pounds of ordnance. Missiles fired included AIM-7M Sparrow, AIM-9M Sidewinder, AIM-120A AMRAAM, AGM-88 HARM and AGM-65 Mavericks.

By 31 October 1998, the seven flight-test aircraft had completed 2,461 flights and flown more than 3,703 hours. By early December the totals had reached 2,621 flights and 3,918.7 hours. In addition, the Super Hornet team had completed flutter flight testing on 23 October - one month ahead of schedule - and successfully completed Operational Test IIB, receiving the highest grade possible.

During flutter flight-testing, which had commenced in March 1996, all flutter tests were flown by the first prototype, F/A-18E1. ITT test pilot Jim Sandberg of Northrop Grumman was at the controls during the October 23 milestone flight. "We have demonstrated through testing that this aircraft has no aero-elastic limitations and is structurally robust" said Sandberg. "We've eliminated one more headache for pilots and the mission planning staff because the Super Hornet can carry any combination of stores at its design speed limit" he continued.

During the 1.7-hour flight, Sandberg successfully completed two limit (VL) speed dives; Limit dives are one of the many test manoeuvres performed during flutter testing. E1 was carrying two AIM-7 Sparrows, two AGM-65E Mavericks and two AGM-154 JSOWs. "Flying VL tests is a challenge… We have to climb as high as we can, go as fast as we can, and then dive, but only to the speed limit and no farther" explained Sandberg.

F/A-18F1 approaches the wire on the USS *Harry S Trumman* during follow on sea trials in March 1999. Boeing

By August 1998, the test team revealed that the Super Hornet had achieved an unprecedented capability with the addition of a re-configurable flight control system, designed to enhance aircraft safety and the pilot's ability to recover control in the event of a loss of the actuator that directs movement of the horizontal-tail control surface. The re-configurable flight control system, one of the Super Hornet's survivability improvements that make it eight times more survivable than the first generation Hornet, replaces the mechanical backup system in first generation Hornets. In addition to the safety improvement provided by flying qualities that are far superior to those of the mechanical backup system, this approach reduced aircraft weight and cost, and increased the reliability of the flight control devices. For the initial flight tests of the system, F/A-18E1 was flown in clean configuration.

Multiple AGM-88 firings were conducted on 3 December 1998, including the first full system live-fire test with forward firing ordnance on F/A-18F2, flying over the NAWC-WD land range at China Lake.

As the Super Hornet neared the end of its three-year EMD phase the F/A-18 AWL (Advanced Weapons Laboratory) was busy completing the validation phase of aircraft computer and software checkout. As part of the overall ITT, the engineers, maintainers and air crew assigned to F/A-18F2 structured several realistic and demanding "live fires" to assess F/A-18E/F final readiness for supporting its operational evaluation conducted by VX-9 (Air Test and Evaluation Squadron Nine).

Beyond demonstrating several new features of the 13E Operational Flight Program the live fires demonstrated the USN's, then, latest missile software in the form of HARM Block 3A and Block 5.

In the lead up to OPEVAL (Operational Evaluation) live fire testing continued at China Lake through January 1999. On 28 January the Super Hornet program demonstrated its Anti-Ship Capability with a Boeing AGM-84 Harpoon Live Fire, F/A-18F2 launched the missile against a moving ship target on the Sea Test Range at the Pacific Missile Test Centre, Point Mugu, California, the missile impacting the target.

The Super Hornet TECHEVAL Weapon System Verification also included a dual Maverick launch in January 1999; F/A-18F2 launching one each of Laser and IR guided Mavericks during a single sortie against M60 and M47 tank targets.

F/A-18F2 is prepared for launch from the USS *Harry S Truman* during follow on sea trials in March 1999. This series of sea trials saw both F model Super Hornets operate from the carrier. Boeing

In February 1999, regression testing of aircraft software version 7.4 commenced. This final EMD version of software was used in the LRIP (Low Rate Initial Production) aircraft.

On 3 March 1999 the Super Hornet commenced the second series of sea trials during which the aircraft, F1 and F2, were put through a series of rigorous carrier suitability tests that pushed the aircraft to limits beyond those expected during normal operations.

Tests conducted included asymmetric weapons carriage, stores separation, single-engine landings, cross-wind take-off and landings and automatic carrier landing system approaches. Test pilot Lt. Commander. Tim Baker described landing the Super Hornet with one engine idling as a "non-event", continuing, "This aircraft has performed superbly… I come from the [F-14] Tomcat community, and these pilots are going to have it comparatively easy."

A highlight of this second round of sea trials was the first night-time carrier launch and recovery of a Super Hornet, conducted on 8 March. The trials concluded on 14 March following which F1 and F2 were ferried from the carrier off the coast of Florida, to Patuxent River.

While both two-seat F model prototypes were conducting the sea trials, F/A-18E1 was demonstrating the Super Hornet aerial refuelling capability in the skies over Patuxent River. During the successful series of flight tests, F/A-18E1 successfully refuelled another Super Hornet, a Lockheed Martin S-3 Viking and an F-14 Tomcat.

For the aerial refuelling mission the Super Hornet is equipped with a Sergeant Fletcher, Inc. ARS (Aerial Refuelling Store), which is an external fuel tank and hose reel mounted on the centreline of the aircraft. Fuel is transferred from the Super Hornet's ARS to another aircraft by deploying the hose, which has a drogue basket on one end.

As of 14 March 1999, the seven flight-test aircraft had completed more than 2,975 flights and flown more than 4,390 flight-hours.

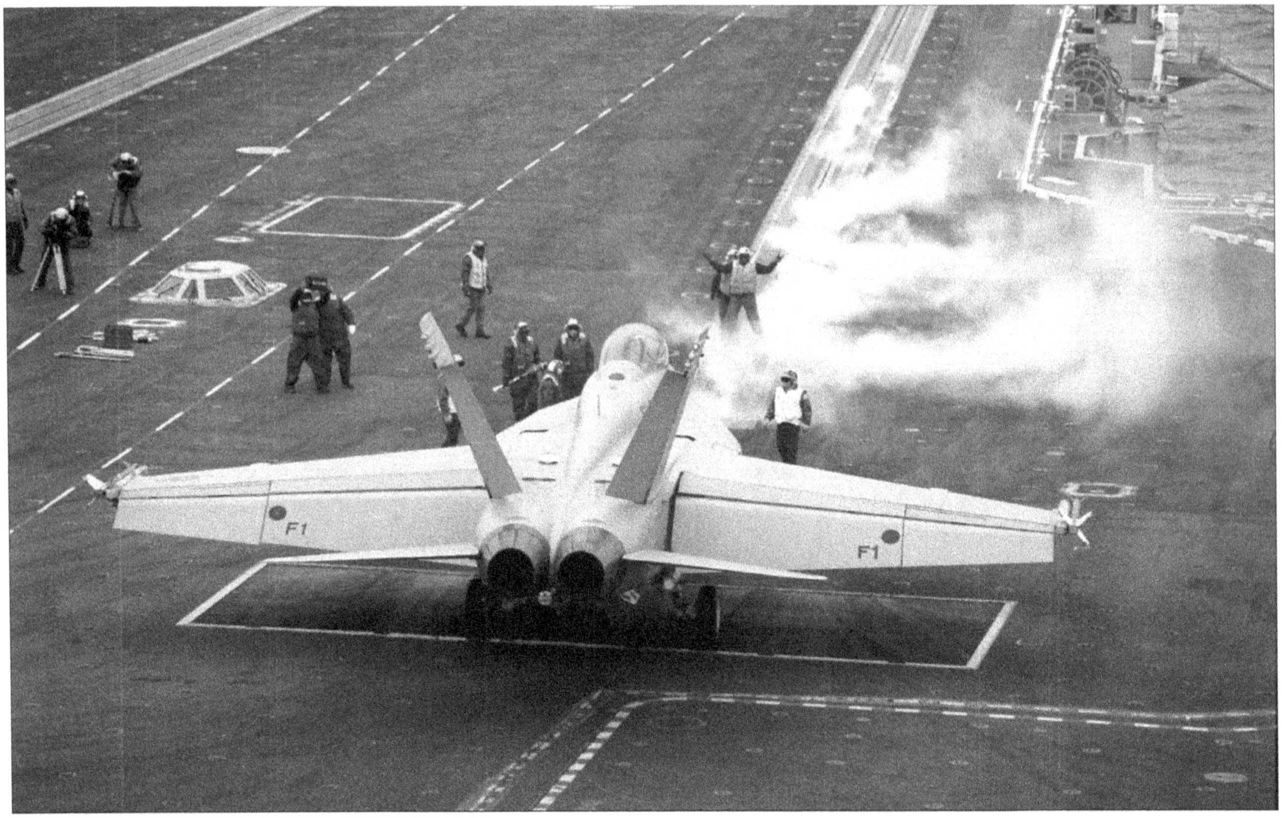
F1
F1

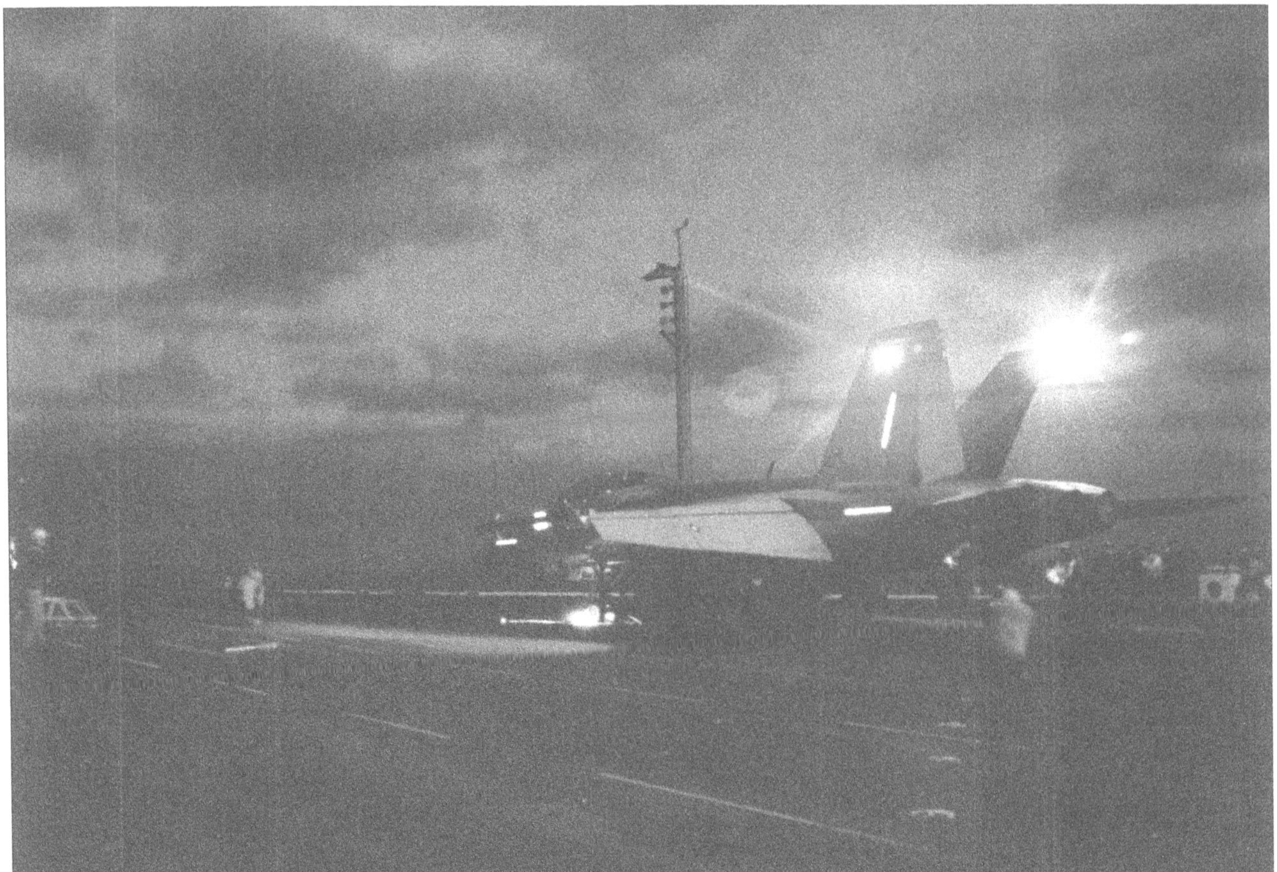

Previous page top: F/A-18F1 is prepared for launch on the USS *Harry S Truman* (CVN 74) in March 1999. Previous page bottom: The follow-on sea trials included the first night-time launch and recovery of a Super Hornet from an aircraft carrier, F1 being launched and recovered on 8 March 1999. Boeing

Above: F/A-18E1 refuels a Lockheed Martin S-3 Viking over the Atlantic Ocean on 11 March 1999. Boeing

F/A-18F2 lifts of from China Lake on the EMD fleet's 500th flight in November 1999. NAWC-WD

Following the sea trials, March 1999 continued to be a busy month for F2, which demonstrated the Super Hornets air-to-air performance, launching two AIM-120 AMRAAM's against unmanned target drones with on over the NAWC-WD, China Lake, range on the 25th. The aircraft also engaged targets with the M61 20-mm cannon. The multi-tasked mission was conducted to verify Air-to-Air capabilities prior to formal delivery of Super Hornets to VX-9 for OPEVAL. Both AMRAAM's and the gunshot were recorded as lethal, the targets being destroyed.

On 30 April 1999, the EMD phase of the Super Hornet test program was successfully concluded. During EMD, the seven development Super Hornets completed more than 15,000 test points, a total of 3,172 flights and 4,673 flight hours in less than three and a half years of flight testing. The following is a brief summary of each development aircraft main contribution to the EMD program:

87

An F/A-18F about to take the wire aboard the *Harry S Trumman* in March 1999. Boeing

F/A-18F2 taxis at China Lake runway for its departure flight in August 1999. F2 flew across the Continental US to join the other prototypes at NAS Patuxent River. NAWC-WD

E1: E-1's primary assignment was envelope expansion and flutter testing. By the end of EMD E-1 had flown a total of 359 flights in 676 hours. Since July 1998, E1 had accomplished testing of four flutter stores loading, completing the EMD flutter program. Flutter testing of 15 external stores loading cleared the aircraft for carriage of all EMD specified stores loading with no aero-elastic speed restrictions. The final two loading configurations incorporated AGM-154 JSOW. Support from the C-130 tanker aircraft was vital to flutter testing, which required high speeds and, thus, high fuel consumption. E1 conducted 638 aerial refuelling.

Following completion of flutter testing, E1 was used to fulfil both baseline test requirements and provide data for technical investigations. E1 accomplished the successful testing of the E/F re-configurable flight control laws following horizontal stabilator failure. E1 also performed tower fly-byes at Webster Field with the purpose of providing source error-correction verification data. Near the end of EMD E1 was involved in mapping the underwing environment by carrying instrumented stores, including JDAM.

E1 was put into flyable storage following its final flight on 1 December 2000.

E2: E2 was primarily assigned to flying qualities, performance and propulsion testing. The first aerial refuelling from a Super Hornet tanker was performed from E2 carrying an ARS using F/A-18B/C models as receiver aircraft. Other aerial refuelling tests were accomplished from KC-135 and KC-130 aircraft to evaluate flying qualities and to verify refuelling quantities and rates.

Propulsion testing included engine inlet distortion and engine operability. Flying qualities testing included verification of flight control computer software loads, forward CG testing, and LEX vent elimination. Performance testing included the usual turn performance points, as well as the w/delta range performance testing. The transonic cleanup flights continued the effort to further understand lateral activity and buffet caused by the wing environment. Various wing configurations were flown, including combinations of thickened trailing edge flaps and ailerons, rows of vortex generators, pylon-mounted stall strips, untoed outboard wing pylons, and production porous wing-fold fairings. Testing in 1999 included transonic flying qualities instrumentation and flying, software version 7.4 regression testing, propulsion distortion and operability cleanup, fuel systems testing, stores drag reduction testing, ARS envelope expansion, and final airplane configuration performance verification.

E3: E3 was the load's survey testing aircraft. Loads survey for the clean aircraft without stores was completed with flight 258 on 22 September 1998. Much of E3's work after that was on loads survey with externals stores, which commenced in July 1998. Other flights were for flying quality evaluation in the clean and external stores configurations, and regression testing for versions 7.2 and 7.3.1 FCS software. Testing through the remainder of the EMD program included the completion of loads survey with external stores, flying qualities evaluation at load-limited flight conditions, dynamic stores release, and assisting with JBD and catapult testing at Lakehurst.

E4: E4 was the high AoA and spin test aircraft. The high AoA testing evaluated the spin recovery and multi-axis input response characteristics of various stores loading, which included aft CG locations and lateral asymmetries. During FCS V 7.3.1 regression testing, a prolonged spin recovery resulted in the high AoA program being put on hold until release of V 7.4 in late January 1999. The flying qualities testing included various cleanup and degraded modes evaluations in fighter and interdiction loading. In addition, propulsion testing was conducted to evaluate inlet distortion, engine/inlet compatibility, and engine operability. E4 went through modification for employment in weapons separation and successfully completed several test events. Remaining work during EMD included air-to-ground weapons separation, as well as high AoA and spin testing following version 7.4 software delivery.

E5: E-5 was the primary weapons separation vehicle. By the first quarter of 2000, E5 had flown a total of 414 flights and 489 flight-hours. E5 and F2 were used during the successful completion of operational testing (OT) IIB conducted at China Lake., which consisted of a variety of air-to-air and air-to-ground missions, including FAC (A), CAS, DAS, BFM, day/night low level, and weapons delivery accuracy. Weapons delivery envelope expansion included Mk 82 BSU 86, Mk 83CFA, Mk 83 BSU 85, Mk 84, GBU 10, Mk 76, Maverick, and HARM. E5 completed separation envelope expansion for Rockeye cluster bombs, AMRAAM and external fuel tanks and conducted envelope expansion for deployable countermeasures (ALE-47 and ALE-50). E5 successfully completed aero-acoustic noise and vibration, and ACLS testing in the fighter escort configuration.

F1: F1 was employed as the carrier suitability test aircraft and, from summer 1998, high AoA evaluations to clear the F model OT-IIB envelope. F1 was also used for OT-IIB pilot high AoA familiarisation flights. Fuel thermal management system ground and flight performance demonstrations were completed, and ATC control law optimisation was conducted. The F1 team also deployed to Edward's AFB for cross-wind landing and ground Vmc tests, accomplished on the dry lake bed runways.

F1 was employed in engine stall investigations at Lakehurst that included JBD run-ups and steam ingestion catapults. Vmc determination for full and half flaps at various AoA's were conducted with several loadings, both symmetric and asymmetric. Maximum asymmetry (30,000-ft-lb) high-sink rate arrestment demonstrations were completed for both the mean pitch attitude and nose-down pitch attitude. Additionally, maximum hook load and maximum off centre arrestment were completed in this loading. F1 and F2 participated in the sea trials in March 1999.

F2: F2 was the primary mission systems aircraft, relocating to NAWC-WD, China Lake, in April 1998. F2 returned to Patuxent River in August 2000, the departure flight being its 615, 446 of which were conducted while at China Lake.

Activities completed at NAWC-WD included the second OT-IIB by VX-9, the first night Super Hornet flight in July 1998; verification program for software suite -13E changes, -13E validation; AIM-9 and AIM-120 live fire launches in June 1998; dual HARM live fire launches against ground threats in December 1998; dual AGM-65 live fire launches

This head-on view of an F/A18F on the deck of the USS *Harry S Trumman* clearly shows to advantage the wings in the folded position. Boeing

against fixed and stationary tank targets and a live fire of an AGM-84 Harpoon against a surface target in January 1999. F2 also dropped live MK82 bombs, (100 tons of free fall ordnance were delivered by F2 while at China Lake) and conducted joint operations with the USMC for execution of close air support procedures. F2 conducted the first ALE-50 deployments in February 1999 and the first carriage of the ATFLIR by a Super Hornet in May 1999. F2 returned to NAWC-AD at Patuxent River in February 1999 to support the March Sea trials deployment before returning to China Lake.

On its return to Patuxent River in August 2000, F2's first assignment was to support maintenance training for Super Hornet engineers of the Strike Aircraft Directorate as part of the FOT&E (Follow On Test and Evaluation) Phase of the Super Hornet program, which followed the EMD phase. The next phase of flight-testing, Operational Evaluation (OPEVAL), with VX-9 commenced in May 1999 and was completed that November (see Chapter 8), with seven of the first batch of 12 LRIP Aircraft.

Following the conclusion of EMD, the flight test aircraft continued to be used in FOT&E, mainly at Patuxent River. EMD was primarily geared toward clearing the basic airframe, weapons and systems necessary for OPEVAL. In FOT&E other objectives were tested for longer-range requirements. Five wet stations, four 480-gal external fuel tanks, smart weapons, JDAM, JSOW and SLAM ER were cleared for separation, loads, flying qualities, etc. The ATFLIR was also being cleared for use during FOT&E.

System upgrades such as the AHRS (Altitude Heading Reference System) and new flight control sensor packages were also evaluated and test time was set aside for deficiency report fixes, OPEVAL concerns and further investigation into transonic flying qualities and testing continued with the ground test airframes.

An F/A-18F is manoeuvred to the catapult during sea trials. Boeing

A live fire fuel ingestion test was conducted on 14 July 199 to evaluate the vulnerability reduction provided to the Super Hornet by the specifically designed inlet ducts built to reduce the leakage rates as a result of a ballistic impact. Additionally, the test was to evaluate the fuel ingestion tolerance of the General Electric F414 engine (a vulnerability that was uncovered during joint live fire tests of the early F/A-18A Hornet deign).

A large armour-piercing incendiary round was used to penetrate through the inlet and into the fuselage fuel tank. Fuel leaking into the inlet was minimal and did not cause any noticeable changes in the F414 engine, which continued running for an additional five minutes without any performance degradation. On 22 October a live projectile was shot into fuel tank number one of test vehicle SV52 at China Lake in a test procedure known as an ullage (trapped fuel) shot. The projectile entered the fuel tank, filled with JP-5 fuel, from above and right, detonating within the tank. The test vehicle suffered only minor damage with some panels coming off the turtleback. The temperatures in the cockpit were not extremely high and the ejection seat survived the event. The mannequin in the cockpit did take a single fragment in the elbow and some fragments hit the ejection seat, but did not penetrate through. The initial indications from this trial were that the pilot could have ejected from the aircraft after fuel tank number one exploded. The test vehicle remained intact throughout the event and there was no inadvertent cockpit seat ejection. Pending a requested waiver of the engine core ballistic shot, the live fire-test objectives for Milestone III were all successfully completed.

In December 1999, F/A-18F2 flew the EMD and follow on test programs 5,000[th] flight-hour during a 1.9 hour flight which was part of the design and development phase for the 18EI mission computer software for future production Super Hornets. F2 had previously flown its 500th sortie in November.

Super Hornet and Hornets line the deck of *the USS Harry S Trumman* during sea trials in March 1999. Boeing **Follow on test and evaluation utilised production Super Hornets as well as the prototypes. This aircraft was involved in high-order language software development.** USN F-18AW
Bottom right: Grainy video frames from the guided JDAM launch from a Super Hornet on August 29, 2001. NAVAIR

As FOT&E progressed more weapons were cleared for use on the Super Hornet. The first flight release of a JDAM from a Super Hornet was conducted on 24 March 2000 when F/A-18F4 released the weapon over the Atlantic Test Range, Patuxent River. On 29 August 2001 the first guided launch of a GBU-31 JDAM from an F/A-18E flown by the NAWC-WD Weapons Test Squadron took place over the China Lake range. Operational capability of the Super Hornet JDAM combination has been given high priority as the weapon is scheduled for the Super Hornets first operational cruise in 2002.

The busy schedule of F/A-18F2 continued into summer 2000 with among other tasks, testing of the ATFLIR. On 8 June 2000, during the aircraft's third flight in support of the ATFLIR program, F2 conducted its 600th flight. Just over two months later F2 was returned to Patuxent River, departing China Lake on 24 August 2000.

Chapter 5

INTO PRODUCTION

F/A-18E6, the first production Super Hornet from LRIP Lot 1, at St Louis prior to its first flight. The Boeing sign in the background had replaced the McDonnell Douglas sign since the roll-out of the prototypes. Boeing

At the time of its inception, development and introduction, the Super Hornet programs importance cannot be underestimated. Not only was it crucial to the USN, which without the Super Hornet would have faced an acute aircraft shortage in the first decade of this century, it was also important to industry all over the USA. Around 7,000 people in St. Louis and some 46,000 nation-wide were employed on the program when the aircraft entered service in 2002.

Boeing would build the forward fuselage and wings, and conduct final assembly; Northrop Grumman was the principal airframe subcontractor, supplying the centre and aft fuselage; General Electric Aircraft Engines produced the F414 engines; and Raytheon provided the radar system in either APG-73 or APG-79 form. In addition, numerous sub-contractors were involved in the program

The USN planned to purchase its first F/A-18E/F's in 1997, at a flyaway unit cost of $36.4 million at 1990 prices. As early as 1993 the USN had planned to request funding for 12, 12 and 48 aircraft in FYs 1997, 98 and 99. These early production figures were altered, and by 1996 it was planned to request funding for LRIP in three Lots of 12, 20 and 30 aircraft in FY's 1997, 98 and 99 respectively.

In mid-March 1997 the US Defence Secretary agreed to delay the decision on LRIP due on 28 March as recommended by the US GAO (General Accounting Office) who said that it would be better to await the outcome of a congressionally ordered weapons project study later that year. A short while later it was revealed that the Defence Secretary had dropped the objections of the GAO and was to proceed with the LRIP decision. Therefore, on 28 March 1997, a DAB (Defence Acquisition Board

A new assembly facility was opened for the Super Hornet in St Louis. Boeing

meeting approved three lots of 12, 20, and 30 aircraft for LRIP, along with LRIP of the General Electric F414 engine, which had been awarded limited-production qualification.

Twenty-seven F414s were purchased for the 12 Lot 1 Super Hornets, with the first production engine delivered in July 1998. Initially production commenced at around three engines per month, although this was to increase to ten per month once the Super Hornet entered full-scale production. Going on the figure of 1,000 Super Hornets under procurement plans at that time, 2,300 F414's were to be purchased through 2017, although this total was substantially reduced following the reduction in aircraft numbers to be ordered.

The FY1997 LRIP batch of 12 aircraft consisted of eight F/A-18E's and four F/A-18F's. By the end of Lot 3 production, production was scheduled to increase to 48 aircraft per year at $48.7 million flyaway unit cost at 1997 prices, excluding the aircraft's integrated ECM suite. With 1997 funding, metal was cut on the first Lot of 12 aircraft and funding for the second lot of 20 was included in the 1998 defence budget.

In May 1997, Northrop Grumman, began centre and aft fuselage assembly for Lot 1 production, followed in September that year by the commencement of forward fuselage assembly by McDonnell Douglas.

After successfully negotiating the LRIP hurdle McDonnell Douglas suffered a setback to the program with the announcement of program cut recommendations by the QDR (Quadrennial Defence Review). Following increasing concerns that the three tactical fighter programs - F-22A, JSF (now F-35) and F/A-18E/F could not be afforded at the then proposed production levels, the US Defence Secretary attempted to avoid outright cancellation

The first production Super Hornet, F/A-18E-6, retracts its undercarriage after take off from St Louis on its maiden flight on 6 November 1998. Boeing

of one or more of the programs by a combination of force reductions, base closures and cuts in unit production of many defence programs.

The Pentagons QDR and the CBO (Congressional Budget Office) analysed the three US fast jet operators requirement for 4,400 new fighters at a total minimum cost of $295 billion between 2004 and 2015. These fighters included 438 F-22A Raptors for the USAF ($70b), 1,000 F/A-18E/F Super Hornets for the USN ($80b), and 2,978 JSF for the USAF, USN and USMC ($144.8b). Congress costed all three programs at around $357 billion, $62 billion more than the quoted $295 billion.

On 7 May 1997, defence officials confirmed that the Defence Secretary was to reduce the number of F-22A Raptor, JSF and Super Hornets to be purchased. The recommended cuts which were proposed to Congress on the 15th saw F-22A numbers reduced from 438 to 339 and Super Hornet numbers reduced from the planned 1,000 to a minimum of between 548 and 785. Although not affected as much as the F-22 or the Super Hornet, the number of JSF's was also cut by the QDR. The total planned US purchase of 2,978 aircraft was cut to 2,852. Note: The above figures have been altered several times since, for e.g. F-22 numbers fluctuated up and down, 187 production aircraft eventually being delivered.

The US Department of Defence fiscal year 1998 budget request was for $251 billion. Of this the USN required $2.1 billion for 20 Super Hornets, and in FY 1999 the USN purchased 30 Super Hornets.

In 1998, the USN saw its future carrier air wing fighter force made-up of 14 air defence F-18F's, 24, multi-role F/A-18E's and 12/14 JSF's. If the F-18FC2W variant was funded, which it was in EA-18G form, then this would eventually replace the EA-6B in the electronic warfare role. In addition, with the passing from service of the KA-6D air refuelling tankers, the Super Hornet would adopt a buddy-buddy tanking role.

The LRIP Super Hornets were built in three lots of 12 (fiscal year 1997), 20 (fiscal year 1998) and 30 (fiscal year 1999), pending the annual approval of Congress. Production authorisation called for the delivery of the first production Super Hornet – an F/A-18E - in late 1998, with production continuing into the second decade of the 21st Century.

A Super Hornet lands on the deck of the carrier USS Abraham Lincoln during sea trials in April 2000. USN

As previously recounted, assembly of the 12 Lot 1 aircraft began in May 1997 with centre and aft fuselage assembly at Northrop Grumman's El Segundo, California plant and the Super Hornet entered LRIP at St. Louis on 15 September 1997, an aluminium bulkhead being installed in the forward fuselage of F/A-18E-6. The bulkhead was installed on top of the keel/drag brace sub-assembly, which forms the foundation for the entire forward fuselage and nose of the aircraft. The sub-assembly was constructed and placed in the tooling in half the time required during the EMD phase of the program.

Final assembly of E-6 began at St Louis on June 19, 1998 when the Northrop Grumman built centre/aft fuselage and the Boeing built forward fuselage were joined. The mating of the two sections was accomplished using laser technology provided by a Nicholson splice tool, a process that not only decreases the time required to mate the two sections, but also enhances the accuracy of the fit, resulting in a near seamless splice.

After completion and ground testing, E-6 conducted its first flight on 6 November 1998, taking off from Lambert International Airport, St. Louis, at 11:56 a.m., with Boeing test pilot Dave Desmond at the controls for flight, which lasted the 1.3 hours. E-6 was delivered to the USN on 18 December 1998. Following acceptance, it was ferried to Patuxent River, Maryland, where it joined the flight test program prior to entering OPEVAL with VX-9 at China Lake.

In late February 1999, Boeing delivered the second production Super Hornet, F/A-18F-3 - the first production two-seater. The third production Super Hornet, F/A-18F-4, was delivered on 16 March 1999. The fourth and fifth production aircraft (both 'F' models) were delivered on 30 April 1999, joining the first three aircraft with VX-9 at China Lake. The sixth production aircraft, an, E-7, which was delivered on 12 June 1999, went to NAS Key West, Florida, where it joined the other production Super Hornets detached there as part of OPEVAL. E-8 was delivered on 25 June and E-9 was delivered on 21 July 1999.

F/A-18F (BuNo.165875), the first series production Super Hornet, outside the Boeing St Louis plant prior to its delivery to the USN on 21 September 2001. Boeing

With deliveries of Lot 1 LRIP aircraft underway, assembly of the second lot of 20 LRIP Super Hornets had commenced in December 1998, the first of these aircraft being delivered in December 1999, funding for the aircraft, 8 F/A-18E and 12 F/A-18F's, having been allocated in April 1998 along with funding for long-lead items for FY1999 production, Lot 3, consisting of 14 F/A-18E's and 16 F/A-18F;s plus associated hardware for completion by 2001.

In 1999, the HASC (House Armed Services Committee) committee recommended $2.9 billion (matching the President's request) for procurement of 36 F/A-18E/F Super Hornets, and a five-year, $15.2 billion multi-year procurement contract for 222 Super Hornets. The recommendation supported the position of the Senate Armed Services Committee on F/A-18E/F multi-year procurement. In October 1999, President Clinton signed the FY 00 Defence Appropriations Bill granting the USN authority for Multiyear procurement of 222 Super Hornets over five years - fiscal years 2000 through 2004, on condition that the Super Hornet successfully completed its then ongoing OPEVAL, which concluded the following Month, paving the way for Milestone III approval to begin full rate production and multi-year procurement. The previous day, 14 February, the OPEVAL report was given to DOT&E [Director Operational Test and Evaluation] who would take the report and turn that into the Beyond LRIP work report – a contract for procurement of 222 aircraft being signed on 16 June 2000, bringing to 284 the total number ordered, of which 22 had been delivered. The first series production Super Hornet, an F/A-18F, was delivered 21 September 2001.

Chapter 6

SUPER HORNET OPERATIONAL EVALUATION

OPEVAL was conducted using the first seven Super Hornets delivered by Boeing, including the first production aircraft, F/A-18E-6, here during its first flight from St Louis on 6 November 1998. *Boeing*

Hanger Five at the NAWS (Naval Air Weapons Station) at China Lake, California, was, between May and November 1999, one of the most important buildings for US naval aviation. It is this building that was home to Air Test and Evaluation Squadron 9 (VX-9) 'Vampires', which had the responsibility of conducting the Operational Evaluation (OPEVAL) of the Boeing F/A-18E/F Super Hornet. The purpose of OPEVAL was to test the aircraft in a realistic operational environment and determine its operational effectiveness as a weapon system as well as its suitability to be maintained and operated by the USN.

VX-9 received its first production Super Hornet when F/A-18F-4 arrived at China Lake on 12 February 1999. F4, the second production two-seat Super Hornet, was used for crew training at China Lake prior to entering OPEVAL in May 1999. NAWC-WD

VX-9 at China Lake, command by USN Captain John V. Stivers, consisted of a 22-member air crew contingent consisting of 14 pilots and eight weapon systems officers. Another 70 USN personnel were responsible for maintaining the seven production Super Hornets delivered to the unit for OPEVAL. Personnel from VFA-122 assisted VX-9, supplying four pilots for OPEVAL.

The first seven production Super Hornets were allocated to VX-9 and the unit received the first of these when F/A-18F-4 arrived at China Lake on 12 February 1999. The aircraft, already painted with the 'Vampires' tail markings, was flown form St Louis to China Lake by Lt. Pete Matisoo of the NWTSCL. F/A-18F-4 was used by VX-9 for crew and maintenance training prior to entering the Super Hornet OPEVAL.

On 30 April, the Super Hornet engineering and manufacturing development program was successfully completed at Patuxent River. On the same day, Boeing delivered the fourth and fifth production Super Hornets (both F models) to VX-9, the aircraft being flown from St Louis to China Lake were they joined the first three production aircraft already at China Lake. The last of the seven aircraft allocated to VX-9 (an F/A-18E) was delivered on 25 June 1999.

VX-9's mission was three-fold: The squadron conducted independent operational tests of Strike weapons systems including strike aircraft, conventional warfare equipment, and electronic warfare equipment; develop tactics and procedures for weapons systems employment; and support the USN/USMC fleet. OPEVAL of the Super Hornet was just one of many operational tests being supported by VX-9.

The China Lake flight line during OPEVAL showing three F/A-18F's. Boeing

Originally scheduled for 1 May 1999, the commencement of OPEVAL was delayed. On 21 May, Rear Admiral Jeffrey Cook signed the "Readiness for OPEVAL" certificate allowing OPEVAL to commence on the 27th. For six months from the start of OPEVAL in May, VX-9 crews put the Super Hornet through a complex variety of tactical missions representing the operational arena.

After VX-9 pilots became qualified in the Super Hornet at China Lake, the squadron took the aircraft to Key West, Florida, for a two-week detachment to evaluate tactics development where they flew missions against adversary aircraft. A second detachment put the Super Hornet through two weeks of day and night carrier operations aboard the aircraft carrier USS *John C Stennis* (CVN 74). Here, VX-9 crews operated and supported the seven Super Hornets as an integrated part of the carrier's air wing, CAW 9. Three of the Super Hornets returned to China Lake on 14 July following completion of carrier qualifications. The remaining four aircraft remained aboard the *Stennis* for more tests and arrived at China Lake on 24 July.

Captain Bob Rutherfurd took over command of VX-9 in August halfway through OPEVAL. Towards the end of August, OPEVAL pilots participated in a "Red Flag" exercise at Nellis Air Force Base, Nevada, along with 60 other tactical aircraft. During the two-week exercise the Super Hornets flew interdiction sorties, fighter escort and defence suppression missions and demonstrated joint interoperability on a large scale.

In September and October the focus was directed toward testing aircraft survivability. The Operational Requirements Document stated that the Super Hornet must provide an improvement in survivability over the currently deployed F/A-18C/D, which apparently has been achieved.

The flight test phase of OPEVAL was concluded at China Lake on 16 November 1999 when Commander Jeff 'Zoil' Penfield, OPEVAL Test Director, flew the last flight. During nearly 6 months of flight-testing, VX-9 put the Super Hornet through a complex variety of tactical missions. The seven Super Hornet aircraft flew 1,233.9 flight hours in over 866 sorties, expending over 420,000-lb of ordnance.

An F-18F at dusk during OPEVAL at China Lake. Boeing

At the conclusion of OPEVAL, five of the Super Hornets used in operational testing and evaluation went to NAS Lemoore to begin the process of training instructors for VFA-122.

With OPEVAL flight testing over VX-9 personnel then spent the next 60 days analysing data in preparation of their report which then went to COMOPTEVFOR (Commander Operational Test and Evaluation Force) with recommendations. COMOPTEVFOR then had 30 days to send the final report to CNO (Chief of Naval Operations). On 15 February 2000, the USN announced the results of OPEVAL, the report awarding the Super Hornet the best possible grade, calling it "operationally effective and operationally suitable", recommending the aircrafts introduction to the fleet. The OPEVAL report specifically cited the aircrafts key enhancing features - growth, bring back, survivability, range and payload - as qualities relative to fleet operational capabilities. As is the case with all such reports, details other than the overall conclusion are classified. Success of OPEVAL was one of the requirements for Milestone III approval to begin full rate production which was authorised a few months later.

Chapter 7

SUPER HORNET IN SERVICE

A Super Hornet development aircraft refuels an F-14 Tomcat off the US East Coast. Super Hornets and Tomcats initially operated together until the later was retired in 2006. Boeing

The end of an era was heralded on 19 December 1996, when the USN's veteran Grumman A-6E Intruder completed its last carrier deployment. On this date the fourteen A-6Es of VA-75 departed the USS *Enterprise* for the last time as the vessel sailed towards its home port, Norfolk Virginia, landing at NAS Oceana, Virginia. Twelve F/A-18C/D Hornets replaced the *Enterprise's* Intruders in the carrier air wing. VA-75 had been the first operational squadron to equip with the Intruder when it received A-6A's in September 1963. The Intruder was finally retired from USN service when VA-196 was stood down in a ceremony held at NAS Whidbey Island on 28 February 1997.

Retirement of the A-6E added another twist to the confusion surrounding procurement of the Super Hornet. Just what aircraft was it be supposed to replace? First it was the cancelled A-12 Avenger II, which itself was designed as an A-6 replacement, therefore, the new Hornet variant had become an A-6E replacement. As the USN wanted around 660 aircraft and was suggesting 340 for the USMC to replace little over 300 A-6's, it attempted to justify the numbers by claiming that the new aircraft would supplement the F/A-18C/D in service. Furthermore, with retirement of the A-6E, the Grumman F-14 Tomcat was assuming a large proportion of the A-6's strike mission, as the only other shipboard fighter, the F/A-18C/D had insufficient range to carry out the long range strike mission.

This F/A-18F from VFA-41 is heavily laden for a refuelling mission over the Western Pacific Ocean on 25 October 2003. USN

With the introduction of the LANTIRN (Low Altitude Navigation and Targeting InfraRed for Night) system the F-14 evolved into an all-weather precision strike platform capable of delivering both 'dumb' iron bombs and precision strike weapons such as the GBU-12/24 Laser Guided bomb units. In early 2001, the F-14B was cleared for operations with the GBU-31 JDAM, followed by JDAM trials with the F-14D in July that year. While evolving into a capable air to surface strike platform the Tomcat retained its air to air and reconnaissance missions and also took on the role of airborne Forward Air Controller, a role demonstrated operationally during operation Allied Force in 1999.

With the strike role in the hands of the F/A-18C/D and F-14 Tomcat, both of which took on roles previously assigned to the A-6E, before it was retired, the Super Hornet was now to supplement the F/A-18C/D and replace the F-14, rather than the A-6E as was originally planned. As well as replacing the Tomcat in the strike role, the USN planned to also replace the F-14 with the Super Hornet in the fleet-air defence/air superiority and reconnaissance roles.

The last catapult launch of a Grumman A-6E Intruder. The Intruder completed its last carrier deployment when the last aircraft from VA-75 catapulted off the USS *Enterprise* (CVN 65) on 19 December 1996. DoD

An F/A-18F lands aboard the carrier USS *Abraham Lincoln* with an F/A-18E and another F/A-18F in the background during sea trials in 2000. USN

When the F/A-18E/F program was revealed in 1991 the USN had a requirement for 660 aircraft, which roughly fell into line with the numbers of A-12's that the service had intended to purchase. At this early stage of the program it was expected that the USMC would purchase the aircraft as a follow on replacement for the first generation Hornets then in service, with up to 340 aircraft being anticipated, increasing the total USN/USMC estimated requirement to 1,000 aircraft. The USMC, however, was never fully committed to the F/A-18E/F program, as purchasing this fighter did not conform to its goal of transitioning to an all STOVL (Short Take-Off and Vertical Landing) strike fighter force early in the 21st century. Once the A/F-X and MRF programs had been cancelled, and the JAST program emerged, leading to the JSF, the Marine Corp saw the STOVL variant of the JSF as its way of attaining an all STOVL strike fighter force. Subsequently the USMC cancelled its requirement for the F/A-18E/F.

When the USMC pulled-out of the program, the USN retained its requirement at 1,000 aircraft, although this included 120 un-funded two-seat C2W variants as EA-6B Prowler replacements. The USN further justified the 1,000 aircraft figure by revealing that it intended to replace the F-14 Tomcat with the two-seat F-18F variant optimised for the air superiority role.

Although the program remained on budget and on schedule it has constantly been criticised by the US GAO, which claimed that the limited improvement in capability over the F/A-18C/D did not justify its $80 billion price tag. In June 1996, the GOA, following a lengthy review of the program, issued a report claiming that the Pentagon would be able to save "almost $17 billion" if it were to abandon the $80 billion 'Super Hornet' program, acquire a smaller number of upgraded F/A-18C/D's and wait until the lower cost JSF was available. At the heart of the criticisms was its claim that the Super Hornet has only marginal improvements in operational capability over the F/A-18C/D. It claimed that the range increase was achieved at the expense of combat performance, and that wind-tunnel tests had revealed complications with some intended weapon loads.

An F/A-18F from VFA-122, with wings folded, prepares for its display at Le Bourget, Paris, in June 2001. H Harkins

The report also questioned the Super Hornets 'stealth' improvements, unit cost and the operational deficiency of the F/A-18C/D. It claimed that the F/A-18C/D could remain viable with minor in service upgrades, but the USN pointed out that the main problem with the 'C/D' concerned the issue of recovery payload. According to the USN the 'C/D' was at the end of its growth potential and that is what brought them to the much larger 'E/F'.

According to the GAO, fitting larger external fuel tanks to increase range and incorporating a strengthened undercarriage would have allowed the 'C/D' to operate with a higher bring home payload capability. The Super Hornet program manager Captain Joe Dyer countered this by pointing out that any significant increase of the F/A-18C/D's landing weight would require strengthening of the internal structure, further increasing the F/A-18C/D's weight. "Increase weight and now the approach speed is to fast. You have to increase wing area, which increases drag, so you have to re-engine the aircraft - that's what led to the development of the 'E/F' design" said Dyer.

The USN had already increased the maximum carrier landing weight of the F/A-18C/D by 450-kg to 15,400-kg, with only a marginal increase in empty weight, which probably encouraged the GAO in its criticisms of the Super Hornet. The increased landing weight brought with it operational restrictions such as requiring a higher wind-over-deck, a shallower approach angle and limits on asymmetric stores carriage.

For the F/A-18C/D the USN set the requirement for first-pass fuel remaining at 1800-kg for day operations and around 2300-kg for night operations. An F/A-18C/D landing on a carrier with a recovery payload of 2500-kg allows 700-kg of weapons to be brought aboard with the daytime fuel reserve of 1800-kg. The F/A-18E/F with the same fuel reserve of 1800-kg can come aboard the carrier with more than 2300-kg of unused weapons at its maximum carrier landing weight.

The GAO report criticisms ultimately fell on deaf ears, the USN claiming it was flawed and remaining committed to the F/A-18E/F, the program being considered vital to the future of US carrier aviation.

At Farnborough International in July 2000, Boeing exhibited an F/A-18F and a full-scale mock-up of its JSF contender (USAF variant). Boeing

In the days of 'dumb' iron bombs Air Wing Commanders could afford to simply order unused ordnance to be dropped in the ocean, but today's precision guided weapons are expensive, therefore, that luxury no longer exists. To indicate the importance of the weapon bring home figures outlined above with the daytime fuel reserve of 1800-kg, the F/A-18C/D would not be capable of landing on the carrier deck while still carrying a single JSOW which weighs in at around 900 kg. The F/A-18E/F on the other hand can come aboard while carrying two such weapons. Going on the above figures it has to be assumed that while carrying JSOW, the F/A-18C/D fuel reserve has been reduced in order that JSOW can be brought back on-board the carrier.

F/A-18E aboard the carrier CVN 72, November 2002. USN

An F/A-18E from VFA-115 is positioned for a catapult launch from CVN 72 in April 2002. USN

As previously recounted, the first seven LRIP aircraft were delivered to VX-9, which received its last aircraft, E-8 in July 1999. With deliveries to VX-9 complete, the remaining LRIP aircraft were allocated to other test and training units within the USN. VFA-122 'The Flying Eagles' was established at NAS Lemoore, California, on 15 January 1999, as the USN's first fleet Super Hornet squadron. VFA-122 was a Fleet Readiness Squadron responsible for air crew and maintenance training in the Super Hornet. When the squadron formed it consisted of about 60 personnel, but grew over the next few years.

Beginning in May 1999, VFA-122 air crew and maintenance personnel began supporting VX-9 with operational testing of the Super Hornet at China Lake. At the conclusion of OPEVAL, five of the Super Hornets used in Operational testing and evaluation went to Lemoore to begin the process of training the instructors for VFA-122. The squadron began receiving its aircraft before the end of OPEVAL when the first Super Hornet for the squadron, F/A-18E-11, was delivered to Lemoore on 20 September 1999, followed by F/A-18E-12.

VFA-122 received a further seven Super Hornets during an arrival ceremony at Lemoore on 17 November 1999. The squadron then received in excess of 34 Super Hornets up to 2001. In June 2000, the first class started flying, crew graduating in early 2001.

Prior to VFA-122 receiving its first Super Hornets, the Test Wing Atlantic at Patuxent River received F/A-18E-10 - the ninth production Super Hornet. E-10 spent around nine months with the F/A-18E/F Integrated Test Team at Patuxent River for instrumentation and testing as part of the Follow On Test and Evaluation phase of the Super Hornet test program.

In summer 2000, E-10 went to Eglin AFB, Florida, for Climatic Chamber Testing. This important milestone for the aircraft was the first time that USN maintainers were completely responsible for a Super Hornet.

The test squadron had flown Super Hornet system integration flights before, teaming with the F-18 AWL (Advanced Weapons Laboratory), since F2 had arrived at China Lake from Patuxent River in 1998. However, E-9 was the first Super Hornet to be directly assigned to the squadron, this aircraft having been delivered to the USN in August 1999.

An F/A-18E from VX-23 aboard the USS *Theodore Roosevelt* (CNV 71) on 9 November 2002. USN

An F/A-18E from VFA-115 catapults off the USS *Abraham Lincoln* (CVN 72) during JTFEX off the US West Coast on 3 May 2002. USN

On 9 November 1999, Boeing delivered the final LRIP 1 Super Hornet, F/A-18E-13, almost two months ahead of the contractual delivery date of 31 December. The aircraft was delivered to Patuxent River for additional testing before being ferried to Lemoore.

The China Lake F/A-18 IPT took delivery of F/A-18E-14, in the second week of December 1999, this being the first Super Hornet from Lot 2 of LRIP.

The aircraft was configured with RFCM (Radio Frequency Counter Measures), PIDS (Positive Identification System), MIDS (Multi-Functional Information Distribution System), DCS (Digital Communication System) and ATFLIR (Advanced Targeting Forward Looking Infrared). There were approximately 24 flights addressing System Configuration Set (SCS) 18Ei and OPEVAL issues conducted between December 1999 and late April 2000. Beginning in May 2000, F/A-18E-14 was grounded for approximately 90 days undergoing further instrumentation modifications, which included AMC&D (Advanced Mission Computer and Displays and TAMMAC (Tactical Aircraft Moving Map Capability). E-14 flew in this configuration until March 2001, at which time it was modified again to accommodate the JHMCS (Joint Helmet-Mounted Cueing System) hardware.

During March 2000, VFA-122 instructor pilots completed their initial carrier landings on the USS *Abraham Lincoln* (CVN 72) off the coast of Southern California. While aboard the *Lincoln*, the squadron was joined by two other Super Hornet teams conducting sea trials. Aircraft and personnel from the ITT and pilots and support personnel from VX-9 were also aboard to conduct testing. In total there were 7 F/A-18E/F's which performed 293 arrested landings on-board the carrier. During work up to the first Super Hornet operational cruise VFA-115 took its aircraft back aboard the USS *Abraham Lincoln* to participate in Joint Forces Exercise off the west coast of the US in May 2002.

While VFA-115 was an F/A-18E heavy squadron, the first F/A-18F squadron was VFA-41, which began the transition to the Super Hornet in November 2001 at Lemoore, with transition completed in April 2002. Aircraft of VFA-41 embarked on the carrier USS *Nimitz* (CVN-68) during June 2002. VFA-41 was the first squadron to be equipped with the ATFIR on an operational cruise.

The next squadrons to transition to the Super Hornet were VFA-14 'Top Hatters' and VFA-102 'Diamondbacks', the latter moving from NAS Oceana to Lemoore to transition from F-14 Tomcats to the Super Hornet. VFA-14 became the first operational (non-Fleet Replacement) squadron to transition to the Super Hornet in early 2002.

Boeing delivered the 100th Super Hornet, an F/A-18F, on 14 June 2002, this aircraft being delivered to VFA-102.

Top: On 14 June 2002, Boeing delivered the 100th Super Hornet, an F/A-18F. Boeing Above: The SHARP pod, here on F/A-18E2, was deployed on the F/A-18F in 2003. USN

The first of 12 F/A-18E's from VFA-115 lands aboard the USS *Abraham Lincoln* (CVN-72) on 24 July 2002. USN

On 24 July 2002, VFA-115 landed 12 F/A-18E's aboard the USS *Abraham Lincoln* (CVN-72) as part of Carrier Air Wing 14 following a 45 minute flight from NAS Lemoore. The carrier then headed across the Pacific with other ships from the battle group to take up station in the Arabian Gulf in support of Operations Southern Watch and Enduring Freedom.

The Super Hornet was tasked with launching ordnance in support of both of these operations. However, with no air to air and no realistic ground to air threat over Afghanistan and facing an obsolete Iraq air defence system over Iraq neither operation was going to be any real test of the Super Hornets capabilities.

Two squadrons of F/A-18E and one squadron of F/A-18F's participated in the March/April 2003 US invasion of Iraq, and two squadrons continued operations over the country helping to enforce the US/coalition occupation of that country.

Figures released show that during VFA-115's deployment from 2002/2003 the aircraft dropped 209,000-kg (460,000-lb) of ordnance on Afghanistan and Iraq. This included 159,000-kg of ordnance dropped during the March/April 2003 invasion of Iraq. The non-production standard ASQ-228 ATFLIR pods deployed with the unit proved unreliable, therefore, the aircraft relied on the AAS-38 targeting pod on the F/A-18C/D to designate targets. The production standard ATFLIR achieved IOC (Initial Operational Capability) with VFA-103 at Lemoore on 10 September 2003.

Ordnance dropped included 900-kg JDAM's, 450 kg LGB's, 250-kg and 450-kg general-purpose bombs and a small number of AGM-145 JSOW's. The 12 F/A-18E's of VFA-115 flew some 5,400-hrs and completed 2,463 arrested landings. During the deployment the Super Hornets had a claimed sortie completion rate of 98% without loss. In reality the biggest threat to the aircraft over both Afghanistan and Iraq was mechanical failure. As mentioned above neither country had any real credible air defence capabilities. Iraq had a number of air defence systems; however, these were completely obsolete and incapable of combating the medium altitude operations conducted over the country by the bulk of coalition air power including the Super Hornets.

At the beginning of April 2003, four F/A-18F's from VFA-41 aboard the USS *Nimitz* (CVN 68) were transferred to the CVN 72 air group to augment tanker support. VFA-115 had configured some of its aircraft as airborne tankers, reducing the number of

110

Top: An F/A-18E on the deck of the aircraft carrier CVN 72 on 24 July 2002. Above: An F/A-18E from VFA-115 lands on CVN 72 off the US Pacific coast on 24 July 2002. USN

Top: An F/A-18E from VFA-115 about to launch from the deck of the USS *Abraham Lincoln* on 20 August 2002. Above: **Hornets and Super Hornets** on the deck of the USS *Nimitz* off the coast of California on 16 September 2002. USN

Top: An F/A-18E from VFA-14 'Tophatters' prepares to launch from a steam catapult on the USS *Nimitz* off the Californian coast on 17 September 2002. Above: An F/A-18E from VFA-115 launches from CVN 72 on 13 September 2002. USN

Top: **An F/A-18F from VFA-41 lands on-board the USS *Carl Vinson*; with another VFA-41 Super Hornet on the flight deck.**
Above: **An F/A-18E from VFA-115 carrying JDAM GPS guided bombs.** USN

During the US March/April 2003 invasion of Iraq the F/A-18E/F's were tasked with air to air refuelling missions as well as strike missions. This VFA-115 F/A-18E, heavily configured with external fuel tanks for the air to air refuelling mission, is seen launching on a mission on 28 March 2003. USN

aircraft available for strike missions. As the campaign progressed tanker configured missions increased from 15-20%. The four F/A-18F's flew over 4,000-miles from the USS *Nimitz*, which was on-route to the Gulf region to relieve the *Abraham Lincoln*. The *Nimitz* had two Super Hornet squadrons as part of her air wing which was the first to deploy with both the F/A-18E and the F/A-18F on board, replacing the two F-14 Tomcat strike fighter squadrons. VFA-15 equipped with the F/A-18E and VFA-41 with the F/A-18F joined the Super Hornets of VFA-115 and the four VFA-41 Super Hornets aboard the *Abraham Lincoln* in conducting missions over Iraq from early April 2003. The F/A-18F's of VFA-41 brought with them production standard ATFLIR pods, which were more reliable than the pods equipping VFA-115, and the SHARP reconnaissance pod, the latter bringing credible reconnaissance capability to the Super Hornet operations.

Block II

While the initial Super Hornet provided a leap in combat capability for US naval air power, it was with the Block II upgrade that the Super Hornet truly evolved into a 21st century fighter. The Main features of the Block II upgrade were provision for the APG-79 AESA, ACS (Advanced Crew Station) with large 200 x 250-mm (8 x 10 in) display and de-coupled cockpits in the F/A-18F, allowing near simultaneous air to air and air to ground operations to be conducted from the rear cockpit. Other features include a digital video map computer, fibre-optic data networks, which has 1,000 times the capacity of the 1553 data-bus, required to carry the radar data. The Harris supplied duel-redundant fibre channel network switches have the capacity to link up to 16 systems including the AESA, SHARP, ASQ-228 ATFLIR, , IDECM, digital video map computer and new mission computers. The idea was for the USN to move away from the practice with the first generation Hornet of introducing new configurations with new production Lots, therefore, having different combat capabilities throughout the fleet. The aim of the Block II upgrade was to limit the number of aircraft configurations, with the capability to "plug in" new upgrades as they become available.

The first F/A-18F Super Hornet with the new nose design to accommodate the APG-79 AESA lifts-off from St Louis. Boeing

There were to be two main Super Hornet configurations. Aircraft up to production Lot 25 were to be built to Block 1 standard, which have nothing "architecturally that is planned for Block 2". Block II would be introduced when full rate production commenced with Lot 26.

Although the first Block II aircraft, with a redesigned forward fuselage, ECP-603, required to accommodate the new APG-79 AESA, was delivered on 2 September 2003, it would not be until 2005 that the APG-79 became available. The APG-79 was flown in a development aircraft on 30 August 2003, followed four days later by the award of a contract for LRIP, the first production AESA being delivered by Raytheon to St Louis on 28 December 2004. The first Block II Super Hornet equipped with the APG-79 was flown on 21 April 2005.

The Block 1 IDECM self-defence suite of the Block I Super Hornet comprised the Raytheon ALR-67(V)3 RWR, Northrop Grumman/ITT ALG-165 jammer and the Raytheon ALE-50 towed Decoy. The definitive Block 3 IDECM for the Block II Super Hornet was designed to include the Northrop Grumman ALQ-214 techniques-generator and the associated ALE-55 fibre-optic towed decoy, a major improvement over the ALE-50. While the latter simply repeats received signals the ALE-55 transmits signals received from the ALQ-214.

A major improvement in the Block II upgrade is the new advanced mission computer and displays. The AMC replaced the AYK-14 mission computer installed in the Block I Super Hornet, a system carried over from the F/A-18C/D. The duel AMC for the Block II Super Hornet is driven by PowerPC processors providing increased throughput, fibre channel high speed data network and software written in the high order C++ language which is easier to use and maintain.

The AMC was developed in two main stages. The AMC Type 1, which was to be retrofitted to Block I aircraft would introduce high order language software running the existing operational flight program translated from assembly language to C++. Block II aircraft AMC utilised a PowerPC G4 processor.

The first MYP Contract was awarded in June 2000 for 222 aircraft through FY2004. The second Super Hornet MYP contract, MYP II, was awarded for 213 aircraft to be delivered through FY2009. In FY 2009 the contract was increased by 44 aircraft, 20 for the USN and 24 F/A-18F's for the RAAF, bringing to 257 the number of aircraft procured under MYP II.

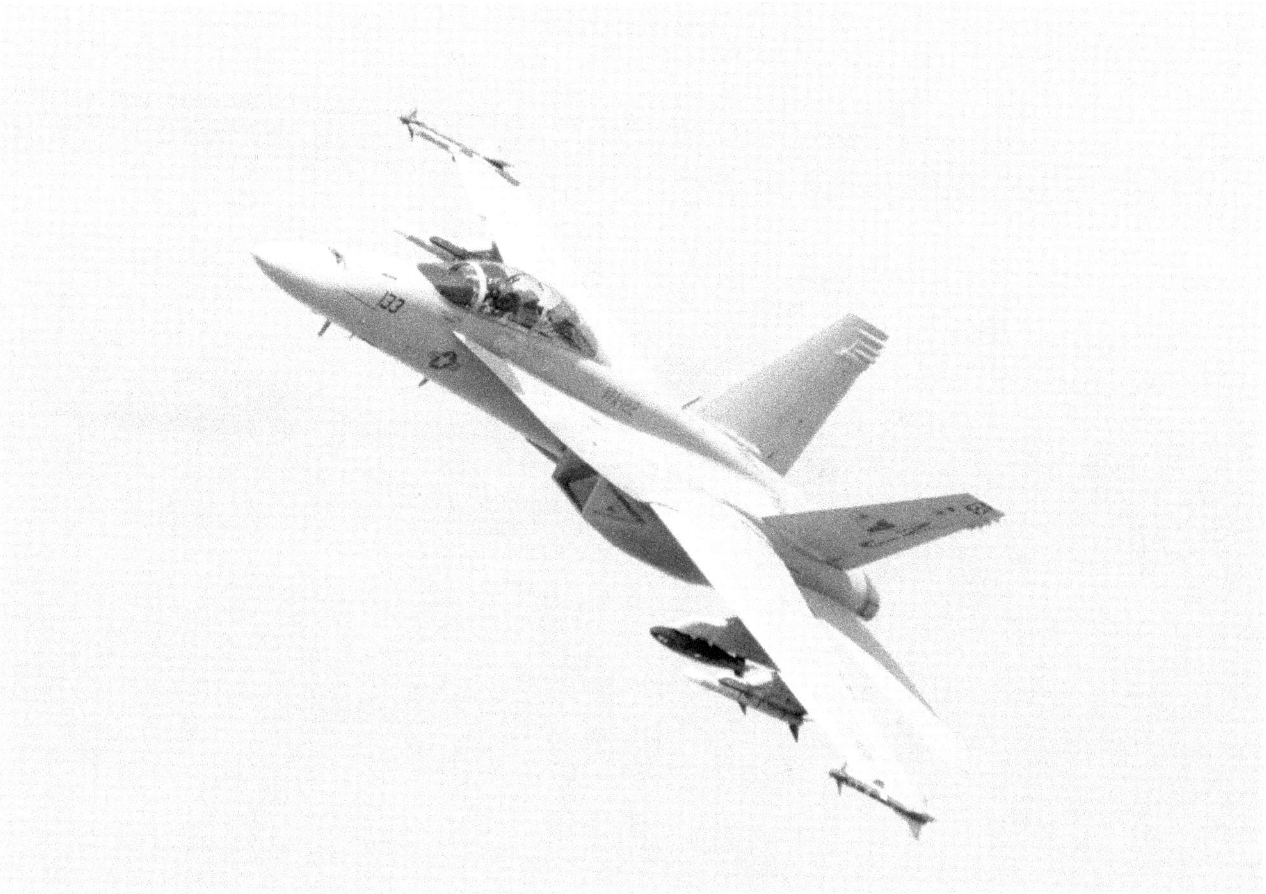
133

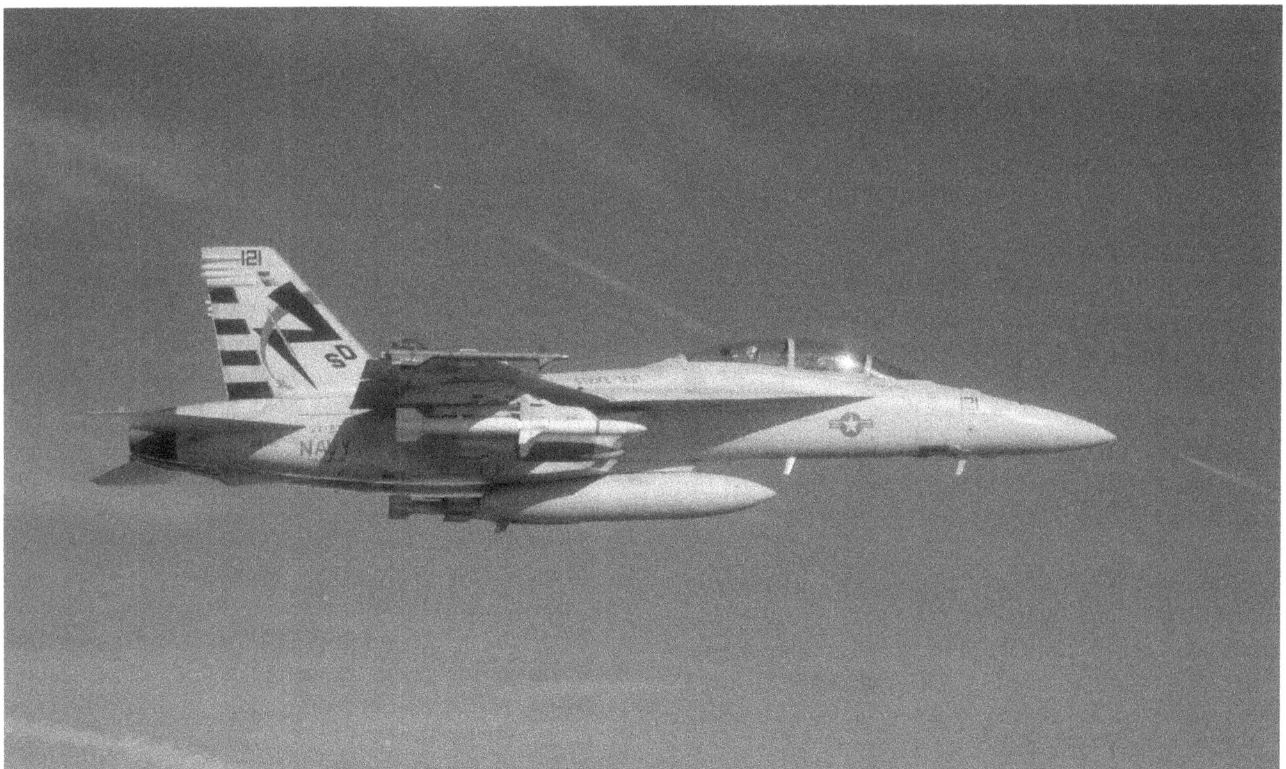
121
NAVY

Previous page: Top: An F/A-18F being flown with air to air missiles and air to free fall bombs. Boeing **Previous page bottom: This F/A-18F, operating with VX-23 (Naval Test Wing Atlantic) is being flown on a 'captive carry' test flight with the Raytheon AGM-88E AARGM.** USN

Above: Vortices stream from the LERX and wingtip's of this F/A-18E from CV 1 USS Carl Vinson (CVN 70) in 2011. USN

The third MYP contract, MYP III, was awarded in September 2010 for 124 aircraft; Super Hornets and EA-18G Growlers. The MYP III initially covered 66 F/A-18E/F's and 58 EA-18G's, but was increased by an additional 24 F/A-18F's, bringing to 148 the number of aircraft procured through this contract. The open contract allows orders to be increased up to 194 aircraft.

The 100th Block I Super Hornet was delivered in June 2002. The first Lot 25 Super Hornet was delivered on 15 October 2002, this Lot introducing the AMC and new displays. The 200th Super Hornet was delivered on 24 August 2004; the aircraft going to VX-9 at China Lake. VFA-106 'Gladiators' at NAS Oceana received its first Super Hornets on 2 September 2004, this Fleet Replacement Squadron being the first East Coast Squadron to receive the them.

In October 2006, VFA-213 at Oceana was the first squadron to be declared operational with Block II Super Hornets, IOC with the Block II being declared in December that year. VFA-22 took the Block II aircraft on its first deployment in May 2008.

The 400th Super Hornet was delivered to the USN on 24 July 2009, and the first aircraft from the MYP III contract was delivered to the USN on 15 March 2011. On 20 April that year the 500th Super Hornet/Growler was delivered to the USN.

The Super Hornet has been regularly deployed in Support of operations in Iraq until 2011 and Afghanistan, ongoing in 2014. By early 2012 the Super Hornet had "logged more than 166,000 … flying hours supporting operations in Iraq and Afghanistan". Operations were flown over Libya in 2011 and in late summer 2014 operations over Iraq commenced again, targeting Islamic State forces which had made sweeping gains in Iraq's de-facto civil war that ensued in the fallout of the coalition invasion in 2003 and departure in 2011.

Top: This was the first Super Hornet to be delivered with a HAL built gun bay door. Above: In co-operation with Kongsberg of Norway, Boeing completed fit trials of an F/A-18F with the Kongsberg JSM (Joint Strike Missile). Boeing

The first F/A-18F, AFA-01, for the Royal Australian Air Force. Boeing

RAAF F/A-18F

With the closure of the F/A-18C/D production line and the lack of surplus airframes, Boeing turned to the Super Hornet to compete in export fighter competitions, but to date only the RAAF (Royal Australian Air Force) has purchased the aircraft.

The export drive began during the aircraft's development. Boeing took a pair of F/A-18F's to the Farnborough International Air Show in July 2000. This first overseas deployment was followed in February 2001 by a pair of F/A-18F's appearing at the Australian International Air Show at Avalon, Victoria. This was the aircraft's longest deployment at that time, requiring assistance from a pair of Boeing KC-135 Stratotankers, and overnight stops at Guam, and Hawaii in the Pacific.

In February 2002, the Australian government asked Boeing for an "unsolicited proposal" for an undisclosed number of Super Hornets to replace the 35 General Dynamics F-111C/G strike aircraft in RAAF service, which were suffering wing structural problems, bringing their projected retirement date forward from 2020 to around 2012. The Super Hornet proposal was separate from the Project Air 6000 project for a replacement for the RAAF F/A-18A/B Hornets, for which the Super Hornet would also be considered, although Australia announced the selection of the Lockheed Martin F-35 Lightning II in 2002.

In May 2007, Australia signed a letter of Offer and Acceptance for the purchase of 24 F/A-18F's and final assembly of the first Super Hornet for the RAAF commenced at St Louis on 17 December 2008, and the aircraft, AFA01, was rolled out on 8 June 2009 and conducted its maiden flight on 14 July that year.

On 28 May 2010, five F/A-18F's arrived at RAAF, Amberley, a further six arriving on 6 July. A further four Super Hornets arrived on 6 January 2011, the same date that No.1 Squadron RAAF achieved IOC on the F/A-18F. Six F/A-18F aircrew and maintenance trainers arrived at Amberley on 9 May 2011, followed by a further five F/A-18F's on 3 August, the final four aircraft, of the 24 ordered, arriving on 21 October 2011.

Top: The first F/A-18F for the RAAF conducted its maiden flight on 14 July 2009. Above: The first batch of five F/A-18F's was delivered to RAAF Amberley on 28 May 2010. Boeing

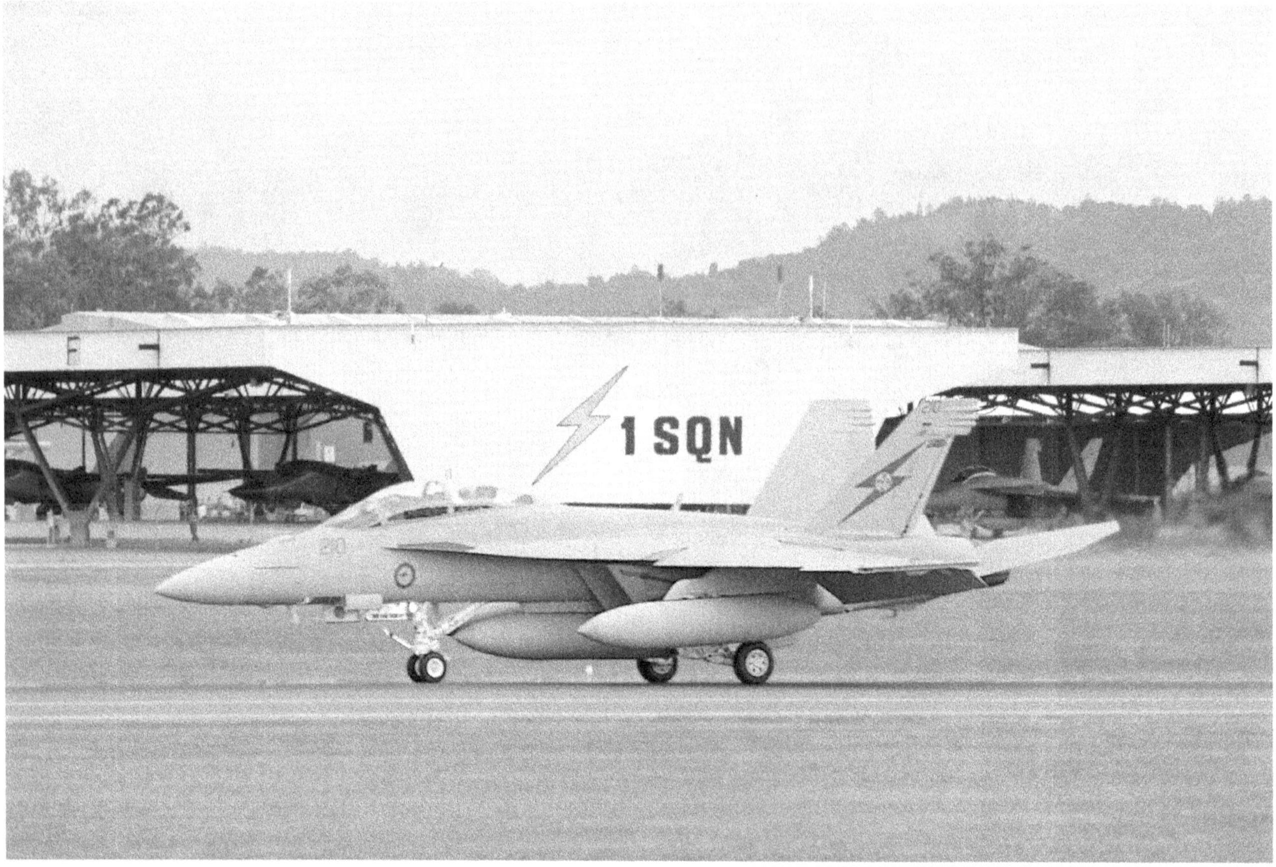
1 SQN

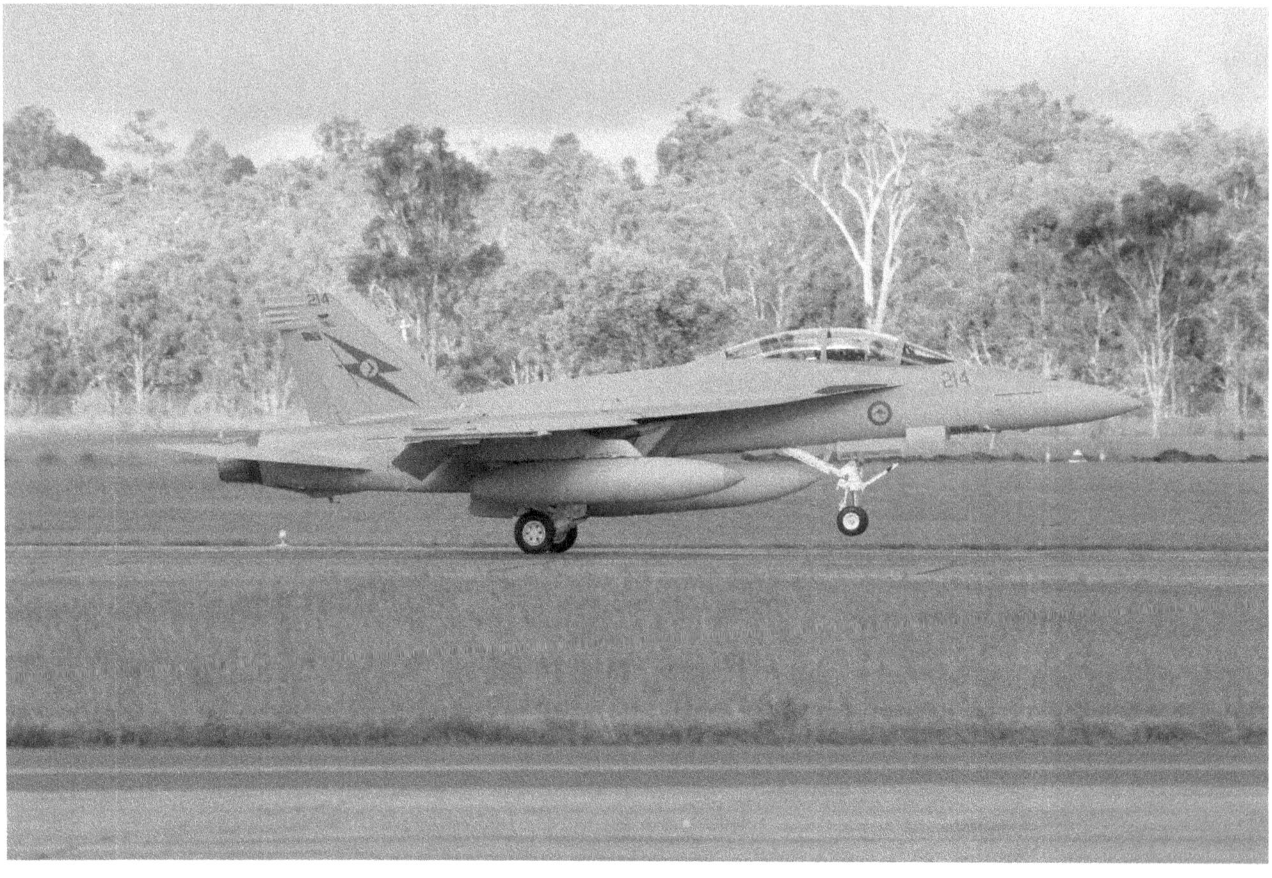

Previous page top: Six F/A-18F's were delivered to Amberley on 6 July 2010. This aircraft rolls past the No.1 Squadron RAAF hanger area containing Super Hornets at right side of photograph and F-111's at left side. Previous page bottom: Four more F/A-18F's arrived at Amberley on 11 January 2011, the same date that No.1 Squadron RAAF attained IOC with the Super Hornet. Boeing

Above: Five F/A-18F's arrived at Amberley on 3 August 2011 and the last four of the 24 Super Hornets ordered arrived on 21 October that year. These aircraft, like aircraft 213 above, were wired to allow them to be converted to EA-18G standard. Boeing

In August 2012, the Australian Government revealed plans to convert 12 Super Hornets to EA-18G Growler standard, wiring for the future conversion being built into the second production Lot of 12 F/A-18F's on the production line, the first of which was rolled out on 23 September 2010.

The Australian F/A-18F's are operated by No.82 Wing; No.1 and 6 Squadrons RAAF. In RAAF service the Super Hornet can be armed with AIM-9X, AIM-7 and AIM-120 air to air missiles, conventional free fall iron bombs, Laser Guided bombs, AGM-84 Harpoon anti-ship missiles and AGM-154 JSOW C, a variant designed to attack hardened land targets. The first AGM-154C launch form a RAAF F/A-18F was conducted in 2014. The Australian aircraft are also certified for use with the AGM-158 JASSM, although this weapon is not operated by Australia.

In late summer 2014 the RAAF F/A-18F's commenced operations against Islamic State targets in Iraq, joining USN Super Hornets and other coalition air assets already committed to operations.

Production totals for the F/A-18E/F amounted to 563 aircraft (including the 24 for the RAAF) along with the seven development aircraft bringing the total to 570, operated by in excess of 30 Squadrons (including test units). In addition there were two EA-18G development aircraft followed by 114 EA-18G production aircraft bringing the combined total to 686 aircraft, although the existing MYP III contract has provision for additional aircraft which had not been ordered in October 2014.

Chapter 8

EA-18G GROWLER AND ADVANCED SUPER HORNET

F/A-18F1 masquerading as the EA-18 demonstrator. Boeing

Even before the official roll out of the Super Hornet prototype, F/A-18E1, the manufactures were turning their attention to other potential variants of the aircraft, and on 7 August 1995 MDC announced that an EW (Electronic Warfare) variant of the aircraft, known then as the C2W, was being studied in co-operation with Northrop Grumman as a private venture using company funding to conduct tests such as wind tunnel testing. No major structural changes were planned, allowing it to be built on the standard Super Hornet production line. The USN directed that the focus be on a more affordable variant which would take advantage of much off-the-shelf technology then being developed for the Northrop Grumman EA-6B Prowler ICAP III upgrade, reducing development costs. Boeing initially proposed adopting the existing ALQ-99 Tactical Jamming System pods employed by the EA-6B.

It was expected that an EA-18 C2W variant would be capable of both radar and electronic communications jamming. The aircraft would also be equipped with a network centric communication system, which would include SATCOM/GPS (Satellite Communication/Global Positioning System), a multifunction information distribution system and advanced data-links allowing it to act as a group leader for other assets in a strike package.

The wingtip pylons could accommodate pods containing wide-band receiving antennas in place of missiles, with the receiver antennas on a removable pallet located in the gun bay, which would require deletion of the internal cannon. Other elements of the electronic warfare suite, including the jamming system, could be carried in pods on the under wing or fuselage stations. The rear cockpit would be mission equipped with a large central tactical-situation display and all mission equipment.

The EA-18 program had its first demonstration flight from Boeing's St Louis facility on 15 November 2001. The aircraft used for the flight was F/A-18F1, which was configured with three ALQ-99 jamming pods, two external fuel tanks and wing tip mounted AIM-9 Sidewinder AAM's. Boeing

Boeing completed two demonstrations of its EA-18 on 20 and 22 August 2002. Boeing

When the EA-18G design emerged, the wingtip stations housed ALQ-218 precision receiver system pods developed from the ICAP III of the EA-6B Prowler. Boeing

Boeing provided the USN with costing for a purchase of 150 EA-18's, which would be based on the Block II upgrade, and on 15 November 2001, completed an initial flight test of the F/A-18F prototype, F1, configured as an EA-18 AEA (Airborne Electronic Attack) variant, as it had become known, configured with three ALQ-99 pods.

By early summer 2003, the USN had revealed plans for the acquisition of 90 aircraft designated EA-18G. The plan called for SDD (System Development and Demonstration) of the Block 1 variant equipped with the ICAP III suite with upgraded ALQ-99 jammer and ALQ-218/LR-700 receiver. The latter system would be repackaged to fit into wingtip pods and the internal 20-mm cannon would be removed to accommodate a pallet containing an AEA suite. In addition to the jamming pods the APG-79 AESA would be capable of jamming in the high-frequency waveband backing up the wide-spectrum coverage of the ICAP III suite.

On 29 December 2003, a 5 year SDD contract was awarded to Boeing, with Northrop Grumman supplying the AEA sub-system for the EA-18G, which was basically an evolved variant of the Block II F/A-18F optimised for the AEA role equipped with the ICAP III (Improved Capability III) system which allows the aircraft to conduct 'selective-reactive and pre-emptive jamming of enemy electronic defences'. Most of the AEA suite is housed in the pallet in the gun bay and on the two wingtip pods. The aircraft retains much of the capability of the F/A-18F Block II ,with nine weapon stations available (the wingtip stations of the Super Hornet are not available), which can be used for combinations of air to air and air to ground weapons, external fuel tanks or additional jamming pods. "The AEA communications receiver and jamming system provide electronic suppression and attack against communication threats." The APG-79 increases electronic warfare capability, being "capable of precision targeting utilizing cues from the ALQ-128 precision receiver system."

An instrumented EA-18G over Patuxent River on 2 August 2006. USN

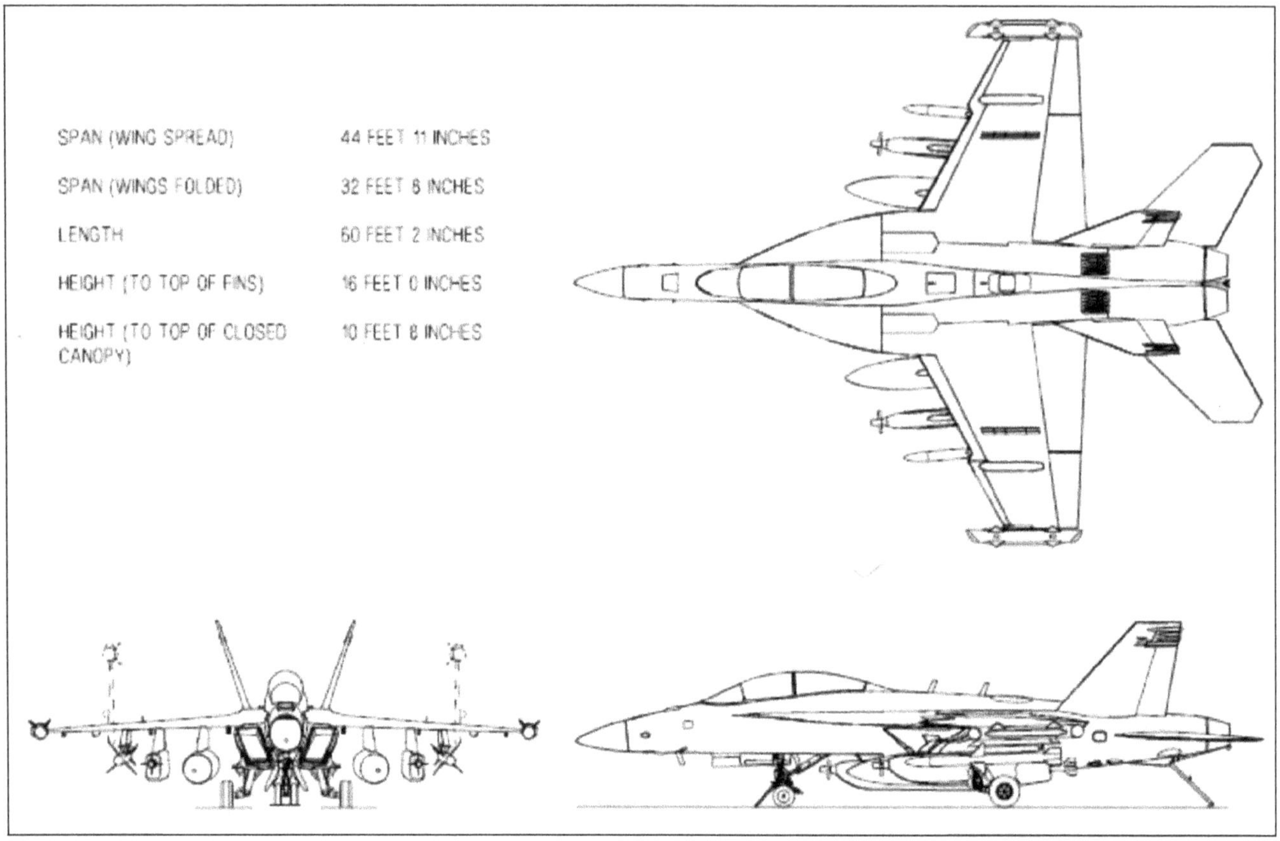

SPAN (WING SPREAD)	44 FEET 11 INCHES
SPAN (WINGS FOLDED)	32 FEET 8 INCHES
LENGTH	60 FEET 2 INCHES
HEIGHT (TO TOP OF FINS)	16 FEET 0 INCHES
HEIGHT (TO TOP OF CLOSED CANOPY)	10 FEET 8 INCHES

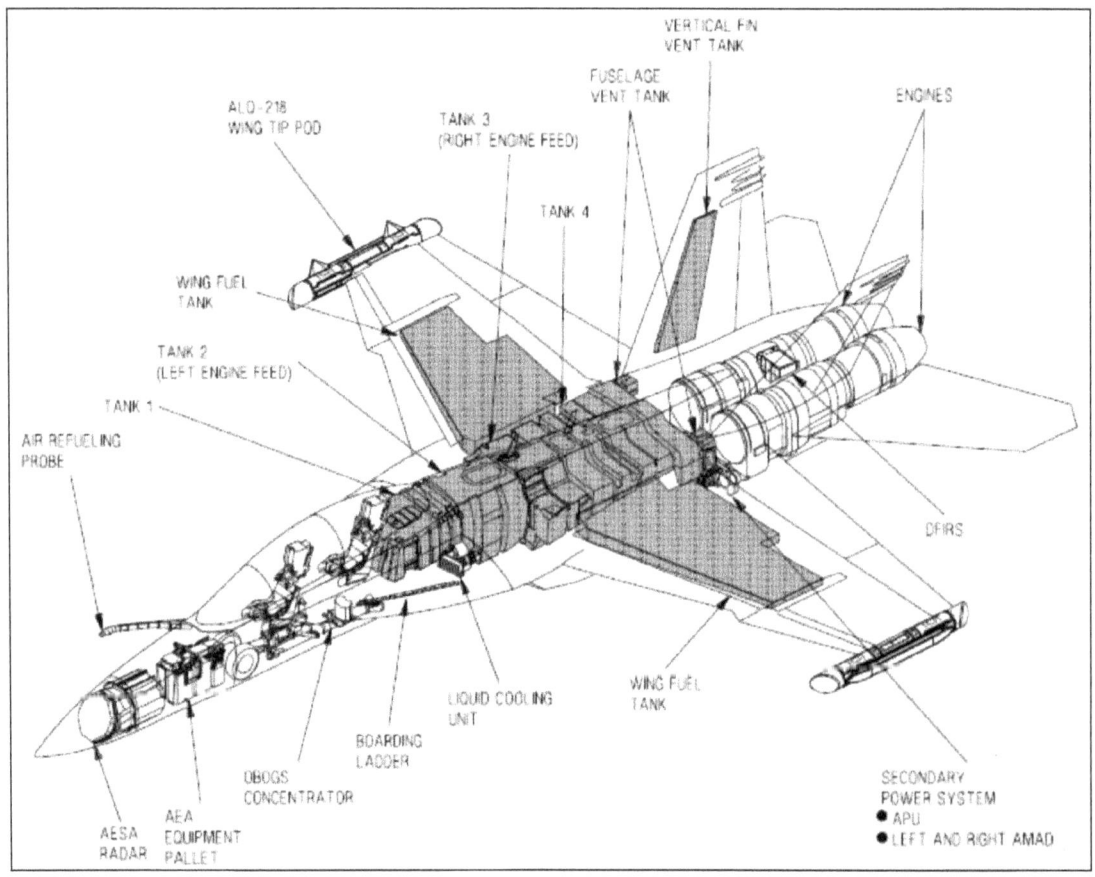

Above: General arrangement three-view of the EA-18G Growler. NAVAIR

Left: Cutaway showing the main areas and systems of the EA-18G. NAVAIR

Top: An EA-18G Growler at NAS Whidbey Island, Washington, in April 2007. USN. Two EA-18G's during SDD flight testing. The aircraft nearest camera is in clean condition except for the wing tip mounted ALQ-218 pods. Boeing

A pair of EA-18G Growlers on a training flight. Boeing

The following brief from Boeing outlines the Growlers capabilities:

- Provides critical electronic intelligence and reconnaissance (ISR) data to other joint force aircraft
- Brings fighter aircraft speed and manoeuvrability to an electronic attack aircraft
- The ability to self protect against adversarial aircraft using its AIM-120 Advanced Medium Range Air-to-Air Missiles
- Enhanced radar image resolution, targeting and tracking range through its APG-79 Active Electronically Scanned Array (AESA) radar system
- Uninterrupted radio communications in a heavily jammed environment using its Interference Cancellation System
- Unequalled aircrew situational awareness and head-up control of aircraft targeting systems and sensors using its Joint Helmet Mounted Cueing System
- The ability to locate, record, play back and digitally jam communications over a broad frequency range using its ALQ-227 Communications Countermeasures Set
- Provides advanced survivability and electronic protection for ground, air and maritime combat forces
- High reliability and lower operating costs

Assembly of the first centre/aft fuselage for the first EA-18, EA-1, commenced at Northrop Grumman on 1 July 2004 and final assembly of the aircraft commenced at St Louis on 22 October that year. EA-1 was rolled out at St Louis on 4 August 2006 and conducted its maiden flight on the 16th of the month. Another development aircraft, EA-2, was built under the SDD contract and four EA-18G's were built in Lot 30 production to support the EA 18G operational evaluation. The first EA-18G production aircraft flew on 10 September 2007 and was delivered to the USN a fortnight later.

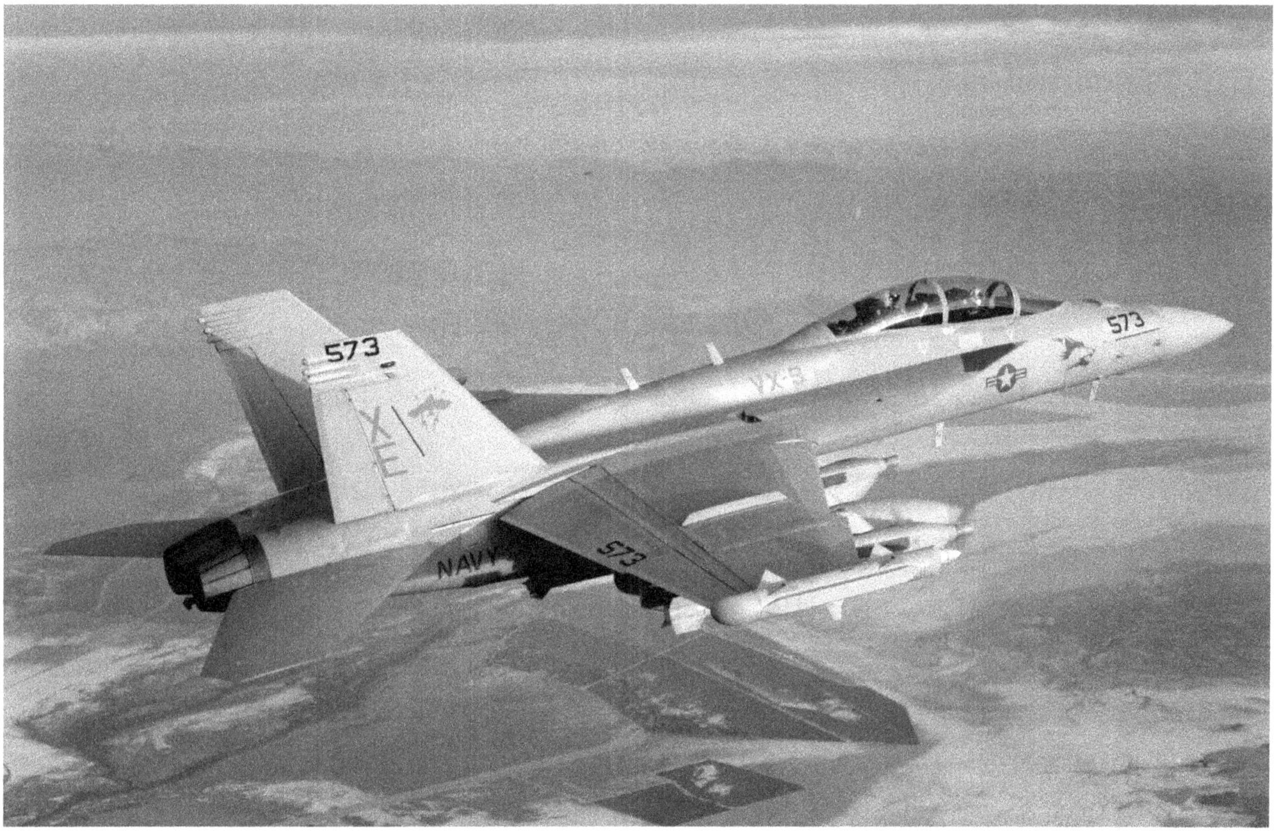
573
XE
573
NAVY
573
573

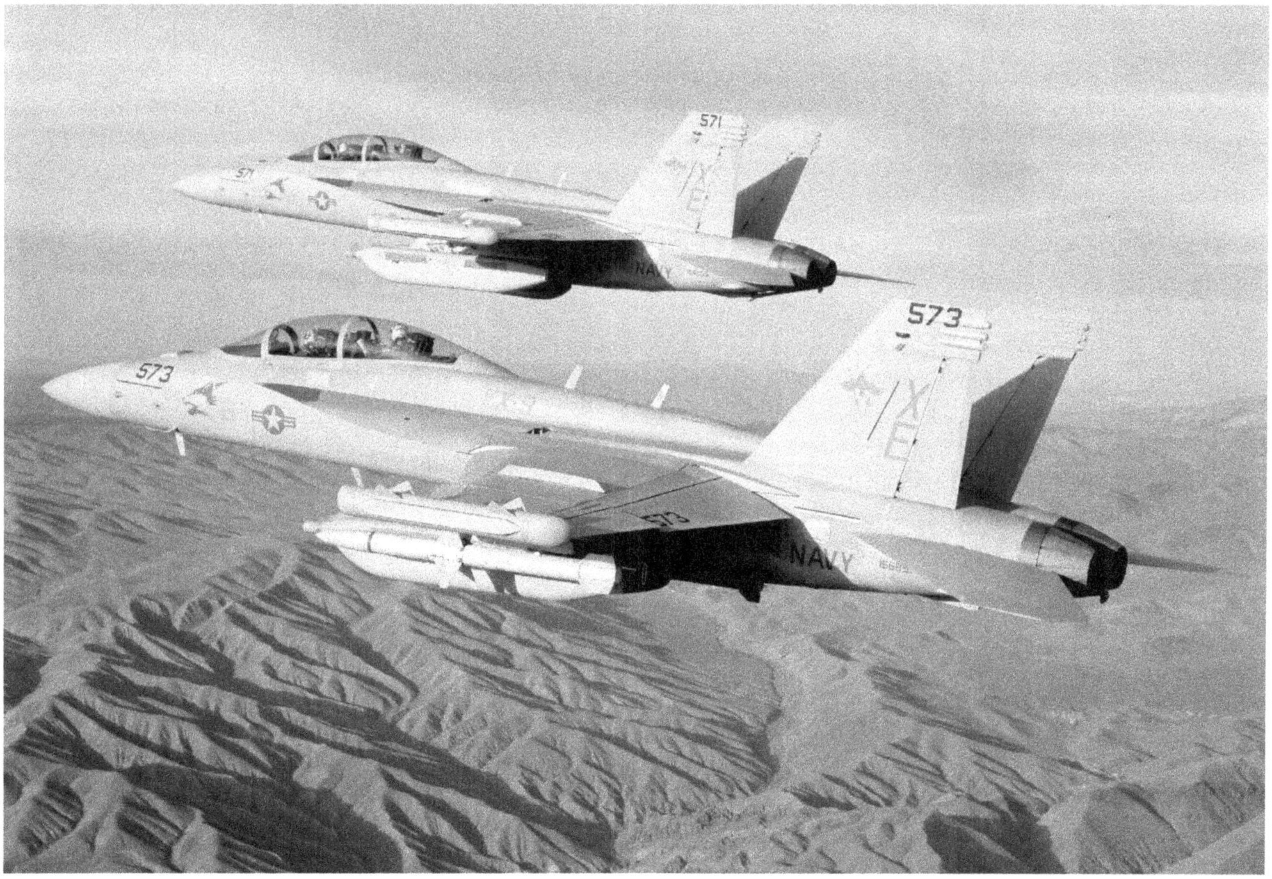
571
XE
NAVY
573
573
XE
573
NAVY

Previous page: Building on the Block II F/A-18F Super Hornet already in service benefited the Growler SDD. Boeing

Above: An EA-18G launches from the USS *Dwight D Eisenhower* during Growler sea trials which were conducted between 31 July and 5 August 2008. USN **Right:** Development EA-18G in a climb during a photo shoot. Boeing

VAQ-129, a Fleet Readiness Squadron, at NAS Whidbey Island, Washington, was the first unit to equip with the EA-18G when it received its first aircraft in August 2008 (Boeing documents state 3 June 2008). Sea trials were conducted aboard the aircraft carrier USS *Dwight D. Eisenhower* in August 2008, the Initial Operational Test and Evaluation was completed in May 2009 and the Growler attained IOC with VAQ-132 at Whidbey Island on 30 September 2009. Full rate production was authorised in November 2009; 114 Growlers being delivered to the USN, the 100th of which was accepted by the USN on 5 May 2014. The Growler force is concentrated at NAS Whidbey Island.

The Growler was deployed operationally over Iraq in 2010 and Libya in 2011, neither deployment being a test of the aircraft's advanced capabilities. Over Iraq the aircraft faced a ZERO electronic threat and over Libya it faced an obsolescent 1970's era defence system which was incapable of combating the modern NATO airpower deployed against it. Available figures show that the EA-18G "logged more than 7,000… flight hours" supporting NATO operations over Libya in 2011 under Operation Odyssey Dawn.

The Advanced Super Hornet, which flew in August 2013, is a continued evolution of the Block II F/A-18E/F Super Hornet/EA-18G Growler. Boeing

Advanced Super Hornet

While the Super Hornet Block II upgrade was under development, Boeing turned its thoughts to what was loosely designated the Block III upgrade, which would look at areas such as reducing the aircraft's radar signature. Among areas being discussed included putting the ATFLIR in the nose of the aircraft.

The program, which would eventually be referred to as the Advanced Super Hornet, was designed to address some of the shortcomings of the Super Hornet to keep the aircraft a viable "A2/AD (Anti-Access/Area Denial)" platform into the 2030+ timeframe. The program is a modular evolution of the existing F/A-18E/F/EA-18G Block II, with all or some of the capabilities designed to be applied to Block II Super Hornet aircraft as retrofits.

The evolution includes signature reduction enhancements, CFT (Conformal Fuel Tanks), EWP (Enclosed Weapon Pod), General Electric F414 Enhanced Engine with a 15-20% thrust increase, Next Generation Cockpit with 11 x 19 in display, integrated intuitive graphics and an internal nose mounted IRST (Infrared Search and Track) system and advanced modes for the APG-79 AESA, including high gain ESM (Electronic Sensor Measures), counter electronic attack and large scale SAR (Synthetic Aperture Radar).

With the CFT, which are designed with a combined 3,500 lb. fuel capacity, the aircraft would benefit from longer range and lower drag. The higher power engines provide increased acceleration, and the program incorporates reduced radar signature enhancements, improved target identification and control off off-board assets and enhanced data fusion "through multi-source integration for information superiority."

Low speed wind-tunnel tests of the CFT (Conformal Fuel Tank) and EWP (Enclosed Weapon Pod) were conducted in March 2012, and Boeing flew the prototype equipped with the CFT and EWP and redesigned nose profile on 5 August 2013, in the first of a planned 21 flights in 31 flight hours to qualify the systems. Over a three week period the flight program stretched to 24 flights, conducted between St Louis and Patuxent River.

The main focus of the Advanced Super Hornet concept was on increasing range and reducing the aircrafts radar cross section to make it stealthier. The conformal fuel tanks are more efficient than underwing tanks and, combined with the EWP, significantly reduce the aircrafts radar signature. Boeing

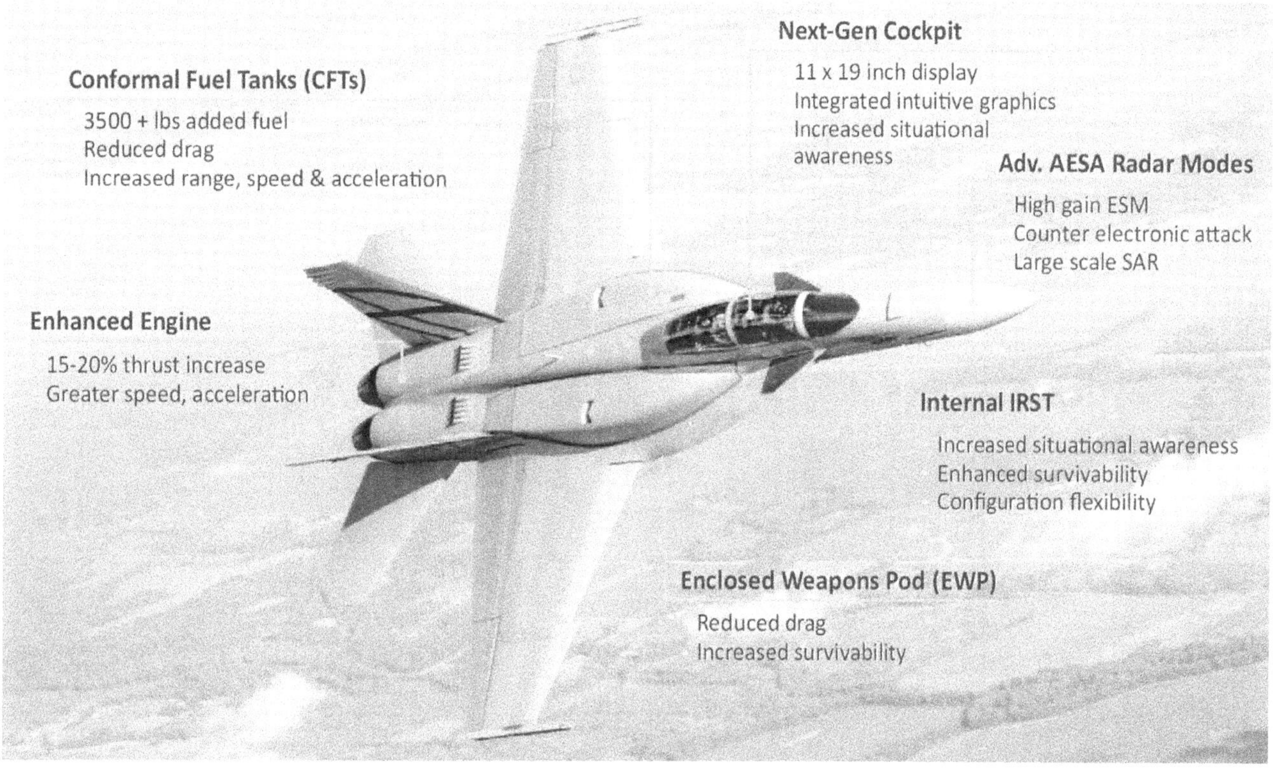

Conformal Fuel Tanks (CFTs)
3500 + lbs added fuel
Reduced drag
Increased range, speed & acceleration

Next-Gen Cockpit
11 x 19 inch display
Integrated intuitive graphics
Increased situational awareness

Adv. AESA Radar Modes
High gain ESM
Counter electronic attack
Large scale SAR

Enhanced Engine
15-20% thrust increase
Greater speed, acceleration

Internal IRST
Increased situational awareness
Enhanced survivability
Configuration flexibility

Enclosed Weapons Pod (EWP)
Reduced drag
Increased survivability

Retouched photograph showing the main points of the Advanced Super Hornet upgrade, which is designed to be introduced on new build aircraft or as a retrofit to existing Block II aircraft. Right: Advanced Super Hornet. Boeing

For the fight test program the CFT and EWP were "configured to collect necessary flight and signature data needed to validate projected performance data." The flight tests concluded that the CFT should increase range by up to 130 nautical miles, increasing combat radius to a distance of over 700 nautical miles. There was a 50% reduction in radar signature compared to the Block II Super Hornet. The CFT configuration proved more aerodynamic than that of under wing external fuel tanks. The EWP allows the carriage of up to 2,500 lb. of stores more stealthily, reducing the time defensive systems have to detect and engage the aircraft.

A number of systems applicable to either the Advanced Super Hornet or the Block II Super Hornet/EA-18G were under test and development in the lead up to the Advanced Super Hornet debut. In September 2010, a combined Boeing USN team flight tested a Distributed Targeting System with Air Test and Evolution Squadron VX-31 at China Lake. On 10 November 2011, Boeing received a contract for development of the Type IV AMC (Advanced Mission Computer) for incorporation into the Super Hornet and Growler, the first series of testing being completed on 10 September 2012. Production of the networked DTS (Distributed Targeting System) for the Super Hornet began in January 2012, and flight tests were completed in early April that year. On 3 June 2012, a SATCOM (Satellite Communications) system was flight tested on a Super Hornet. On 22 September 2011, a $135 million contract was issued for development of the internal IRST under the Advanced Super Hornet program, a contract for the Super Hornet IRST, to be installed in the front end of the centreline external fuel tank, being issued on 22 November that year. The IRST, which was tested on a King Air test bed aircraft in 2013 before being flight tested on an F/A-18F in February 2014, is scheduled for IOC in 2017.

In early 2014, flight testing of the IRST21 on an F/A-18F commenced, the system having been flown on a King Air test bed aircraft in 2013. Boeing

SUPER HORNET & GROWLER PROGRAM CHRONOLOGY

7 January 1991: Pentagon announces cancellation of the General Dynamics/McDonnell Douglas A-12 Avenger II subsonic stealth strike aircraft for the USN.
January 1991: MDC proposed an upgraded F/A-18 Hornet to fill the void created by the A-12 cancellation.
5 May 1992: The US Department of Defence gave the go-ahead for development of the F/A-18E/F.
June 1992. MDC was awarded an Engineering Manufacture and Development contract for the F/A-18E/F.
24 May 1994: Work commenced on the prototype, F/A-18E1/165164
23 September 1994: A second Hornet production line was opened for manufacture of the F/A-18E/F.
May 1995: The McDonnell Douglas built forward fuselage of E1 was joined to the Northrop Grumman built rear fuselage by a computer controlled laser-guided alignment system.
May 1995: General Electric delivered the first flight-ready F414 engine.
7 August 1995: McDonnell Douglas announced that an agreement had been signed with Northrop Grumman for development of the C2W variant of the F/A-18F.
September 1995: General Electric received flight qualification for the F414 engine.
18 September 1995: F/A-18E1 was rolled out at St Louis.
29 November 1995: F/A-18E1 conducted its maiden flight.
26 December 1995: The second prototype, F/A-18E2/165165, made its first flight from St Louis.
14 February 1996: F/A-18E1 was delivered to the NAWC-AD at Patuxent River, Maryland.
19 February 1996: F/A-18E2 was delivered to Patuxent River.
March 1996: The program received first Department of Defence Acquisition Excellence award.
March 1996: Super Hornet flutter flight-testing began.
1 April 1996: The first two-seat F/A-18F prototype, F1/165166, made its first flight.
12 April 1996: E1 achieved the first Super Hornet supersonic flight, achieving Mach 1.1.
13 April 1996: E1 achieves a speed of Mach 1.52.
April 1996: Go-ahead for procurement of Low Rate Initial Production long lead items.
April 1996: McDonnell Douglas and Northrop Grumman team to develop a plan to have an electronic warfare variant of the two-seat F/A-18F achieve initial operational capability between 2007 and 2009.
14 May 1996: Test program surpasses 100 flight hours.
21 May 1996: F1 delivered to Patuxent River.
22 May 1996: F/A-18E2 completes the longest single flight to date, five hours duration.
13 June 1996: Test program surpasses 100 flights.
26 June 1996: Test program surpasses 200 flight hours.
2 July 1996: The fourth single seat prototype, E4 (actually the third 'E' model to fly) made its first flight from St Louis.
July 1996: The ITT wins the Order of Daedalian Weapon System award for 1995. The award is presented annually to recipients in the Army, Navy or Air Force who have made major contributions to the development of an outstanding weapon system.
5 August 1996: F1 performed the first steam ingestion catapult launch of a Super Hornet from NAF Lakehurst.
22 August 1996: E4 was delivered to Patuxent River.
22 August 1996: Test program surpasses 300 flight hours.
27 August 1996: F/A-18E5 made its first flight from St Louis.
30 September 1996: Test program surpasses 400 flight hours.
11 October 1996: F/A-18F2 made its first flight from St Louis.
29 October 1996: Test program surpasses 500 flight hours
October 1996. USN and USMC pilots evaluated the F/A-18F C2W variant in a simulator at Patuxent River.
October 1996: The Super Hornet wins the Aircraft Design award from the American Institute of Aeronautics and Astronautics.
November 1996. The entire Super Hornet test fleet was grounded following a problem with the F414 engine.
December 1996: Test program completes 586.5 flight hours.
18 January 1997: F1 began the Super Hornets first carrier qualification phase, operating from the USS *John C Stennis*.

22 January 1997: F2 was delivered to Patuxent River.
23 January 1997: F1 returned to Patuxent River following its carrier qualification deployment.
1 February 1997: E3 was delivered to Patuxent River, being the last of the seven prototypes to join the test program.
19 February 1997: First stores separation tests conducted when E2 dropped an empty 480-gal external fuel tank from altitude of 5,000 ft.
26 February 1997: A Super Hornet makes successful first flight with three 480-gallon fuel tanks, two Mk 84 bombs, two AIM-9 Sidewinders and two AGM-88 HARM.
28 March 1997: CNO Admiral Jay Johnson flew with Commander Tom Gurney in F2.
March 1997: Weapons separation tests, including single, paired, multiple and ripple configuration tests commenced. Weapons included SLAM, Harpoon, Mk 82, and 480-gallon tanks, separated from both centreline and wing stations.
3 April 1997: All seven prototypes flew on the same day for the first time with some aircraft flying three times for a total of 13 sorties.
5 April 1997: The first missile firing of the program occurred on this date when E5 launched an AIM-9 Sidewinder.
5 April 1997: F2 launched AIM-120 AMRAAM.
1 May 1997: Successful completion of the drop test program.
13 May 1997: test fleet reaches 1,000 flight hours.
May 1997: Northrop Grumman began centre and aft fuselage assembly for Lot 1 production aircraft.
29 August 1997: 1,500th flight-hour flown by F/A-18E1.
August 1997: Super Hornet begins barricade engagement testing.
12 September 1997: 1,000th test flight flown by Super Hornet F/A-18E4.
15 September 1997: McDonnell Douglas (Boeing) began forward fuselage assembly for Lot 1 production aircraft.
20 November 1997: First operational test (OT-IIA) completed
5 December 1997: AIM-9 wingtip and AIM-120 fuselage missile launches completed.
8 December 1997: 2,000th flight-hour flown by F2.
6 January 1998: First inner-wing tool loaded at Boeing
25 February 1998: F1 ferried to Lakehurst, New Jersey, for carrier suitability tests
23 March 1998: F1 completes carrier suitability tests.
March 1998: LRIP II production funding approved along with LRIP III advanced procurement funding.
April 1998: F/A-18F2 moves to China Lake
19 June 11998: First production Super Hornet fuselage joined
13 August 1998: General Electric delivered the first F414 production engine.
August 1998: OT-IIB completed.
August 1998: Full-scale fatigue test airframe (FT50) completed its first lifetime of testing at St. Louis.
23 October 1998: E1 completes EMD flutter flight test program.
31 October 1998: The seven flight-test aircraft had completed 2,461 flights and flown more than 3,703 hours.
6 November 1998: F/A-18E-6 completes first flight.
9 November 1998: Flight test program completes the 2,500th flight
13 November 1998: E-6 entered the new Boeing paint facility in St. Louis.
18 December 1998: F/A-18E-6 was delivered to the USN more than a month ahead of schedule.
December 1998: Assembly of the second lot of 20 low-rate initial production Super Hornets began.
February 1999: Boeing delivered the second production Super Hornet, F/A-18F-3, the first production two-seat Super Hornet, to the USN as scheduled.
3 March 1999: The second round of sea trials began with F1 and F2 aboard the USS *Harry S Truman*.
8 March 1999: First night time Super Hornet carrier landing.
14 March 1999: Second round of sea trials completed.
16 March 1999: The third production Super Hornet, F/A-18F-4, was delivered to the USN.
30 April 1999: EMD was concluded and the fourth and fifth production Super Hornets, F-5 and F-6 were delivered to the USN.
27 May 1999: OPEVAL commenced at China Lake.
12 June 1999: The sixth production Super Hornet, F/A-18E-7, was delivered to the USN.

25 June 1999: The seventh production Super Hornet, F/A-18E-8, was delivered to the USN.
14 July 1999: A successful Live Fire test was conducted at China Lake.
21 July 1999: The eighth production Super Hornet, F/A-18E-9, was delivered to the USN.
18 August 1999: On 18 August the Naval Strike Aircraft Test Squadron at Patuxent River, Maryland accepted Super Hornet F/A-18E-10, the ninth production Super Hornet. This aircraft is the first production model to be owned by Test Wing Atlantic.
23 August 1999: F/A-18E-9 was delivered. E9 was the first Super Hornet delivered to the Naval Weapons Test Squadron, China Lake (NWTS-CL).
20 September: VFA-122 received its first Super Hornet when F/A-18E-11 was delivered to NAS Lemoore.
22 October 1999: The live fire test team at China Lake successfully completed a live projectile shot into fuel tank one on test article SV52.
October 1999: President Clinton signed the FY 2000 Defence Appropriations Bill granting the Navy authority for multiyear procurement of 222 Super Hornets over five years.
9 November 1999: Boeing delivered the final LRIP 1 Super Hornet, F/A-18E-13, two Months Early.
16 November 1999: The flight test phase of OPEVAL was concluded.
17 November 1999: VFA-122 received a further seven Super Hornets during an arrival ceremony at Lemoore.
November 1999: Boeing selected Raytheon to develop the Advanced Electronically Scanned Array radar for the Super Hornet Block II.
November 1999: The Advanced Targeting Forward Looking InfraRed pod was flown on an F/A-18D.
November 1999: F/A-18F2 flew its 500th sortie.
13 December 1999: The first production Super Hornet from LRIP Lot 2 was delivered ahead of schedule when the China Lake F/A-18 IPT took delivery of F/A-18E14.
December 1999: F/A-18F2 flew the EMD test fleets 5,000th flight-hour.
14 February 2000: The National Aeronautics Association announced that the Super Hornet was being awarded the Robert J. Collier Trophy.
15 February 2000: The USN announced the results of the Super Hornet Operational Evaluation conducted by VX-9 at China Lake. The Super Hornet received the highest grade possible.
24 March 2000: The first flight release of a Boeing Joint Direct Attack Munition was conducted when F/A-18E released a JDAM over the Atlantic Test Range at Patuxent River.
6 May 2000: The Super Hornet team received the US aerospace industries highest honour, the 1999 Robert J. Collier Trophy.
8 June 2000: F/A-18F2 conducted its 600th flight.
16 June 2000: Boeing was awarded an $8.9 billion multi-year contract for the production of 222 Super Hornets. This brought to 284, the number of Super Hornets ordered of which Boeing had delivered 22. The 29 aircraft, including the seven prototypes had flown over 9,200 hours by mid-June 2000.
24 August 2000: F/A-18F2 departed China Lake, returning to Patuxent River.
March 2001: Low rate initial production contract for 15 ATFLIR pods.
April 2001: Flight testing of the Super Hornet with the JHMCS commenced.
29 August 2001: Production JHMCS was flown in an F/A-18F.
24 September 2001: Boeing delivered the first full rate production Super Hornet, an F/A-18F, to the USN. This was also the first production Super Hornet delivered with the JHMCS.
15 November 2001: F/A-18F1 conducted its first demonstration flight as a C2W (EA-18) demonstrator.
February 2002: The Australian government asked Boeing for an "unsolicited proposal" for an undisclosed number of Super Hornets to replace the 35 General Dynamics F-111 strike aircraft in RAAF service.
14 June 2002: Boeing delivered the 100th Super Hornet, an F/A-18F.
24 June 2002: Raytheon delivered the first three EMD SHARP pods to the USN.
24 July 2002: The F/A-18E commenced its first operational deployment when the 12 F/A-18E's of VFA-115 landed aboard the carrier USS *Abraham Lincoln* (CVN 72).
15 October 2002: The first Lot 25 production Super Hornet was delivered.
30 August 2003: APG-79 AESA flown in a Super Hornet
2 September 2003: First Block II Super Hornet, with a redesigned forward fuselage, ECP-603, required to accommodate the new APG-79 AESA, was delivered.

29 December 2003: Five year SDD contract was awarded to Boeing, with Northrop Grumman supplying the AEA sub-system for the EA-18G.

1 July 2004: Assembly of the first centre/aft fuselage for the first EA-18G, EA-1, commenced at Northrop Grumman.

24 August 2004: The 200th Super Hornet was delivered.

22 October 2004: Final assembly of EA-1 commenced at St Louis.

28 December 2004: The first production APG-79 AESA was delivered by Raytheon to St Louis.

21 April 2005: The first Block II Super Hornet equipped with the APG-79 was flown.

2005: Second Super Hornet MYP contract, MYP II was awarded for 213 aircraft to be delivered through FY2009. In FY 2009 the contract was increased by 44 aircraft, 20 for the USN and 24 F/A-18F's for the RAAF, bringing to 257 the number of aircraft procured under MYP II

4 August 2006: EA-1 was rolled out at St Louis.

16 August 2006: EA-1 conducted its maiden flight.

May 2007: Australia signed a letter of Offer and Acceptance for the purchase of 24 F/A-18F's.

10 September 2007: The first EA-18G production aircraft was flown.

17 December 2008: Final assembly of the first Super Hornet for the RAAF commenced at St Louis

8 June 2009: First F/A-18F for RAAF was rolled out.

14 July 2009: First F/A-18F for RAAF conducted its maiden flight.

24 July 2009: The 400th Super Hornet was delivered.

20 September 2009: The EA-18G achieved IOC.

28 May 2010: Five F/A-18F's arrived at RAAF, Amberley for the RAAF.

September 2010: The third MYP contract, MYP III, was awarded for 124 aircraft; Super Hornets and EA-18G Growlers.

15 March 2011: The first aircraft from the MYP III contract was delivered to the USN.

20 April 2011: The 500th Super Hornet/Growler was delivered to the USN. Growlers.

22 September 2011: A $135 million contract was issued for development of the internal IRST under the Advanced Super Hornet program, a contract for the Block II Super Hornet IRST, to be installed in the front end of the centreline external fuel tank, being issued on 22 November that year.

21 October 2011: The final four F/A-18F's for the RAAF were delivered.

10 November 2011: Boeing received a contract for development of the Type IV AMC (Advanced Mission Computer) for incorporation into the Super Hornet and Growler.

March 2012: Low speed wind-tunnel tests of the CFT and EWP for the Advanced Super Hornet were conducted.

2013: The IRST, for the Super Hornet was tested on a King Air test bed aircraft.

5 August 2013: First flight of the Advanced Super Hornet demonstrator.

February 2014: IRST flight tested on a Super Hornet.

APPENDICES

APPENDIX I

Variants

F/A-18E prototypes: five development prototypes E1 to E5.
F/A-18F prototypes: two development prototypes F1 and F2
F/A-18E LRIP 1/2/3: 62 - 30 F/A-18E and 32 F/A-18F
F/A-18E/F MYP I/II/III: 501 (including 24 F/A-18F's for the RAAF)
EA-18G Development aircraft: 2 aircraft, EA-1 and EA-2 taken from F/A-18F production
EA-18G MYP II/III: 114
Advanced Super Hornet: One development aircraft evolved from the Block II Super Hornet

APPENDIX II

Boeing F/A-18F Block II

Origin: McDonnell Douglas Corporation (taken over by Boeing in 1997)
Type: Multi-role strike fighter
Powerplant: Two x 96.87-kN (22,000-lb) class General Electric F414-GE-400 low bypass afterburning turbofan engines
Length: 18.3 m (operator documentation states 18.3 m but some documentation has stated 18.4 m)
Height: 4.9 m
Wingspan: 13.62 m with wingtip mounted missiles and 12.76 m without wingtip mounted missiles
Wing area: 46.45 m sq. (500.00 sq. ft.)
Aspect ratio: 3.51;
Weight: 13387 kg standard and 29,900 kg maximum take-off, maximum carrier landing weight 19476-kg (42,900-lb)
Speed: Mach 1.6 (1960 km/h)
Range: 1000 km plus on interdiction mission, 740 km combat radius and 2700 km ferry range without in-flight refuelling.
Ceiling: 50,000 ft.
Fuel: 6531 kg Internal and up to 4436kg external
Weapon load: Maximum load 8051 kg (7,750-lb). Can include free various combinations of air to air and air to surface weapons including free fall 'iron bombs' GBU laser guided bombs, missiles and the internal 20 mm six barrelled M61A1 20-mm cannon mounted in the nose.
G-limits: -3/+9
Crew: Two
Operators: USN and RAAF

EA-18G

Generally the same as F/A-18F Block II except in the following main areas
Weight: 15011 kg empty
Wingspan: 13.7 m with wingtip mounted pods
Range: 1570 km (fully armed and carrying ALQ-99 Low and High band jamming pods and external fuel tanks)

Note: The above details are taken from operator's documentation. In USN documentation Max speed is stated as Mach 1.8

GLOSSARY

AAAM	Advanced Air to Air Missile
AARGM	Advanced Anti-Radar Guided Missile
ACF	Air Combat Fighter
AEA	
AESA	Active Electronically Scanned Array
AGM	Air to Ground Missile
AHRS	Altitude Heading Reference System
AIM	Airborne Interception Missile
AMLCD	Active Matrix Liquid Crystal Display
AMRAAM	Advanced Medium Range Air to Air Missile
AoA	Angle of Attack
ARS	Aerial Refuelling Store
AShM	Anti Ship Missile
ASM	Air to Surface Missile
ASPJ	Airborne Self Protection Jammer
ASRAAM	Advanced Short Range Air to Air Missile
ASW	Advanced Strike Weapon
ATA	Advanced Tactical Aircraft
ATARS	Advanced Tactical Airborne Reconnaissance System
ATF	Advanced Tactical Fighter
ATFLIR	Advanced Targeting Forward Looking Infra-Red
AWL	Advanced Weapons Laboratory
AuTA	Automatic Target Acquisition
BVR	Beyond Visual Range
BVRAAM	Beyond Visual Range Air to Air Missile
C2W	Command and Control Warfare
CALCM	Conventional Air Launched Cruise Missile
CAP	Combat Air Patrol
CASOM	Conventionally Armed Stand-Off Missile
CBO	Congressional Budget Office
CEM	Combined Effects Munitions
CEP	Circular error Probability
CG	Centre of Gravity
COTS	Commercial Off The Shelf
DAB	Defence Acquisition Board
DAF	Dial-A-Function
DCS	Digital Communication System
DECD	Digital Electronic Colour Display
DEMVAL	Demonstration Validation
DERA	Defence Evaluation Research Agency
DFRC	Dryden Flight Research Centre
DoD	Department of Defence
DSD	Digital Systems Development
ECM	Electronic Counter Measures
ECCM	Electronic Counter Counter Measures
EMD	Engineering & Manufacturing Development
EOA	Early Operational Assessment
EPE	Enhanced Performance Engine
EW	Electronic Warfare
FAC	Forward Air Control
FADEC	Full Authority Digital Engine Control
FLIR	Forward Looking Infra-Red
FOT&E	Follow On Test and Evaluation
GAO	General Accountant Office
GBU	Guided Bomb Unit
GE	General Electric
GNC	Guidance Navigation and Control
GPS	Global Positioning System
HARM	High Speed Anti-Radar Missile
HASC	House Armed Services Committee
HMSS	Helmet Mounted Sighting System
HNSC	House National Select Committee
HOTAS	Hands On Throttle and Stick
HTS	Harm Targeting System
HUD	Heads UP Display
IDECM	Integrated Defensive Electronic Countermeasures
IFF	Identification Friend or Foe
IFS	Integrated Flight Simulator
ILS	Instrument Landing System
IMU	Inertial Measurement Unit
INS	Inertial Navigation System
IR	Infrared
IRLS	Infra-Red LineScan
IRST	Infra-Red Search and Track
ISA	Inverse Synthetic Aperture
ITT	Integrated Test Team
JASSM	Joint Air to Surface Stand-Off Missile
JAST	Joint Advanced Strike Technology
JDAM	Joint Direct Attack Munitions
JHMCS	Joint Helmet Mounted Cueing System
JSF	Joint Strike Fighter

JSOW	Joint Stand-Off Weapon	TARPS	Tactical Airborne Reconnaissance Pod System
LANTIRN	Low Altitude Navigation and Targeting Forward Looking Infra-Red for Night	TRD	Towed Radar Decoy
		TRN	Terrain Reference Navigation
LCDS	Liquid Crystal Display Screen	TSSAM	Tri-Service Stand-off Attack Missile
LERX	Leading Edge Root Extension	TWS	Track While Scan
LRIP	Low Rate Initial Production	UK	United Kingdom
LWF	Light Weight Fighter	US	United States
MAG	Marine Air Group	USAF	United States Air Force
MDC	McDonnell Douglas Corporation	USMC	United States Marine Corp
MFD	Multi-Function Display	USN	United States Navy
MFDS	Multi-Function Display Screen	V/STOL	Vertical/Short Take-Off and Landing
MIDS	Multi-Function Information Distribution System		
MoU	Memorandum of Understanding		
MRF	Multi-Role Fighter		
MTBF	Mean Time Between Failures		
NACF	Naval Air Combat Fighter		
NAF	Naval Air Facility		
NAS	Naval Air Station		
NASA	National Aeronautic and Space Administration		
NATO	North Atlantic Treaty Organisation		
NAWC-AD	Naval Air Warfare Centre-Aircraft Division		
NAWC-WD	Naval Air Warfare Centre-Weapons Division		
OPEVAL	Operational Evaluation		
OT	Operational Testing		
P3I	Pre-Planned Product Improvement		
QDR	Quadrennial Defence Review		
RA	Raid Assessment		
RAF	Royal Air Force		
RAAF	Royal Australian Air Force		
RAM	Radar Absorbent Material		
RFCM	Radio Frequency Counter-Measures		
RHWR	Radar Homing and Warning Receiver		
RWR	Radar Warning Receiver		
SAR	Synthetic Aperture Radar		
SCAS	Shortened Control Actuation System		
SCS	Software Configuration Set		
SEAD	Suppression of Enemy Air Defences		
SLAM	Stand-off Land Attack Missile		
SLAM ER	Stand-off Land Attack Missile Expanded Response		
STOL	Short Take-Off and Landing		
TAMMAC	Tactical Aircraft Moving Map Computer		

ABOUT THE AUTHOR

Hugh, a historian and author, has published in excess of forty books; non-fiction and fiction, writing under his own name as well as utilising two different pseudonyms. He has also written for several international magazines, whilst his work has been used as reference for many other projects

www.ingramcontent.com/pod-product-compliance
Lightning Source LLC
Chambersburg PA
CBHW080603170426
43196CB00017B/2893